Microwave Cooking · Baking & Desserts

Litton Microwave Cooking Products, Minneapolis, Minnesota

from Litton

CERTIFIED FOR
MICROWAVE COOKING

LITTON
Microwave
Cooking
Center

CREDITS:

Design & Production: Cy DeCosse Creative Department, Inc.
Author: Barbara Methven
Home Economists: Jill Crum, Cindy Sampson, Lori Adsem
Food Stylists: Muriel Markel, Janna Arnold, Wynn Gubrud, Jean Mitchell
Photographers: Michael Jensen, Steven Smith
Production Coordinators: Bernice Maehren, Nancy McDonough, Mary Sweet
Consumer Tester: Judith Richard
Color Separations: Weston Engraving Co., Inc.
Printing: Moebius Printing Co.

This is no ordinary recipe book. It's like a cooking school in your home, ready to answer questions on the spot. Step-by-step photographs show you how to prepare food for microwaving, what to do during cooking, how to tell when the food is done. A new photo technique shows you how foods look during microwaving.

The foods selected for this book are basic in several ways. All microwave well and demonstrate the advantages of microwaving. They are popular foods you prepare frequently, so the book will be useful in day-to-day cooking. Each food illustrates a principle or technique of microwaving which you can apply to similar recipes you find in magazines or other cookbooks.

This book was designed to obtain good results in all brands of ovens. Techniques may vary from the cookbook developed for your oven. If rotating foods is unnecessary in your oven, that technique may be eliminated. All foods are cooked at either High or 50% power (Medium). The Defrost setting on earlier ovens and Simmer setting on current ovens may be used when Medium is called for. This simplifies the choice of settings while you become familiar with the reasons why different foods require different power levels.

Microwaving is easy as well as fast. The skills you develop with this book will help you make full and confident use of your microwave oven.

The Litton Microwave
Cooking Center

Contents

What You Need to Know Before You Start

Good techniques and the proper utensils are important for baking success. Read the recipe before you start to make sure you have all the ingredients needed. Do not adjust or substitute ingredients like flour, sugar, shortening, liquid, eggs or leavening, which are necessary to the product's structure. Spices, nuts, whole chocolate chips or raisins are the type of ingredients which can be substituted or omitted. Recipes in this book were formulated for microwaving and cannot be used for conventional baking.

Start with a bowl large enough for easy mixing without spilling over the top.

Grease the inside of a liquid measuring cup before measuring molasses, syrup or honey to prevent it from sticking to the sides.

Measure tablespoons and teaspoons in a standard measuring spoon, not ordinary kitchen spoons. For accuracy, fill to heaping and level off across the top with a straight edge.

Use standard, nested measuring cups for dry and solid ingredients. These cups measure accurately when they are full to the top, so they can be leveled off with a straight edge.

Select liquid measuring cups, which have a rim and spout.

above the top measure, for liquids and oil. Set the cup on a level surface, fill to the correct marking, and stoop to read the measurement at eye level.

Keep the electric mixer in a convenient place. Different types of baked products require different amounts of mixing and handling. Read recipes carefully to avoid over or under mixing. Mixer speeds in this book are based on a standard 10 or 12 speed mixer. A hand mixer may need a slightly higher speed, depending on the power of the motor.

Choose clear glass or plastic dishes for microwave baking whenever possible to help you check for doneness in center bottom, which is the last place to finish baking.

Know your Ingredients & How to Measure Them

Ingredients are important to the structure of baked products. Each serves a special purpose. If you make substitutions you may alter the chemistry of the food and produce a poor result. Use fresh ingredients and maintain the right proportions by measuring correctly.

Flour is the basic ingredient in baking. Most recipes in this book call for all-purpose flour. Use the flour recommended in the recipe. Sifting is not necessary. Spoon flour lightly into a nested type measuring cup to overflowing. Level across top with straight edge.

Sugar adds texture, flavor and tenderness. Use the type called for in the recipe. Do not substitute syrup, molasses or honey.

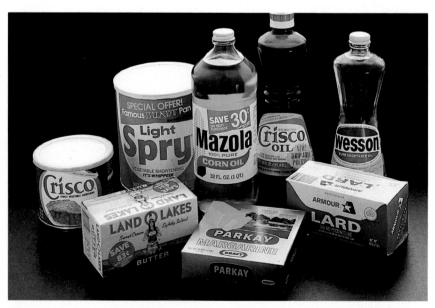

Shortening makes baked goods tender. Hydrogenated vegetable, butter, margarine, lard and oil are all shortenings, but they are not interchangeable. Each has special characteristics.

Use hydrogenated vegetable shortening when a recipe calls for shortening. Use other shortenings only when named specifically in the recipe.

Three Types of Leavenings

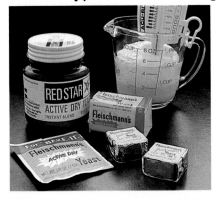

Yeast is a living organism which "feeds" on sugar. At the proper temperature it produces a gas which causes bread dough to rise. Yeast comes in pre-measured packets and cakes and in bulk.

Baking powder is a chemical leavening agent used in quick breads and cakes. It loses its power, so date the can and discard after a year. Heap in standard measuring spoon and level off with straight edge.

Soda is used as a chemical leavening with sour milk or buttermilk in spice, chocolate and fruit based cakes as well as quick breads. Heap in a standard measuring spoon and level off with straight edge.

How to Measure Sugars

Spoon granulated sugar lightly into nested type measuring cup. When overflowing, level off across top with straight edge of knife or metal spatula.

Pack brown sugar firmly into nested type measuring cup. It should hold its shape when turned out. If lumpy, soften as directed on page 7.

Spoon confectioners' sugar lightly into nested type measuring cup; level off across top. Press lumpy confectioners' sugar through sieve.

How to Measure Shortening

Pack solid shortenings into a nested type measuring cup; level off across top. Butter or margarine can also be measured by sticks.

Measure oil in a glass or liquid measuring cup set on level surface. Read at eye level.

Ingredients, continued

Eggs bind ingredients together and give body to baked goods. Recipes in this book use large eggs. Measure if you substitute another size. One large egg equals a scant ¼ cup.

SMALL   MEDIUM   LARGE   X-LARGE   JUMBO

Liquids dissolve sugar, salt and leavening to develop the starch and gluten in flour. Some liquids also add nutrition and flavor. Use liquid measuring cup set on a level surface and check at eye level.

Applesauce, mashed bananas, grated carrots and other fruits and vegetables also provide liquid in some recipes.

Tips for Using Chocolate Chips

Pure chocolate chips are made from chocolate and cocoa butter. When melting with shortening, always use vegetable shortening.

Chocolate flavored chips do not contain artificial chocolate. They are made with cocoa and vegetable shortening. They are stiffer than pure chocolate when melted. Add 1 or 2 tablespoons of vegetable shortening to soften.

How to Use the Microwave as a Baking Aid

Melt chocolate. Microwave at 50% (Medium) 2 to 4 minutes; stir after half the time. To soften pre-melted chocolate, microwave in envelope 10 seconds at High.

Melt chocolate chips. Place measured amount in small bowl. Microwave at 50% (Medium) 2½ to 4 minutes, or until most chips appear soft and shiny. Stir well. If you use chocolate flavored chips, melt 2 tablespoons vegetable shortening with each cup.

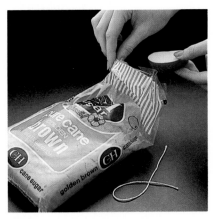

Melt shortening, butter or margarine when recipe calls for it. Starting temperature determines time. Try 1 minute at High, then add more time, if needed.

Heat or boil liquids. For warm liquid, microwave a few seconds. To boil a cup of cold tap water, microwave 1 to 3 minutes. Never boil milk; heat only to scalding.

Soften brown sugar. Place apple slice in bag. Close tightly with string or strip of plastic. Microwave 15 seconds at High or until lumps soften.

Defrost frozen fruit. Remove one metal end from package. Set upright in oven. Place all-paper package on plate. Microwave at High 1 to 3 minutes, or until slightly icy. Do not over-defrost.

Flame desserts. Place 2 to 4 tablespoons brandy in small dish. Microwave at High 15 to 20 seconds to warm. Pour into ladle; ignite and pour over dessert.

Appetizers

Home-baked appetizers add excitement to a party menu. This section offers three pastries to be served as crackers or with hot dips below, plus a genuine made-from-scratch deep dish pizza. The pizza can also be served as a main dish.

Hot Cheese Chip Dip

4 slices bacon, cut in ½-in. pieces*
¼ cup chopped onion
1 cup shredded American cheese

⅛ teaspoon chili powder
Wheat Chips or Rye Chips, page 10, crackers or crisp vegetable relishes

Makes ¾ cup

Place bacon in 1-qt. casserole or small microwave-proof bowl. Microwave at High 2 to 3 minutes, or until almost crisp, stirring once. Drain off fat. Stir in onion. Microwave at High 2 to 3 minutes, or until onion is golden, stirring once. Sprinkle with cheese and chili powder. Do not stir.

Microwave at 50% (Medium) 1½ to 3 minutes, or until cheese is melted, rotating ¼ turn every 30 seconds. Serve hot with chips, crackers or vegetables.

*½ cup chopped ham or cooked sausage meat may be substituted for the bacon. Sauté onion in 1 tablespoon butter or margarine. Or omit meat and substitute ½ cup chopped green pepper. Sauté onion and green pepper in 2 tablespoons butter or margarine.

◀ Gourmet's Delight Chip Dip

1 can (14 oz.) artichokes (not marinated), drained
1 cup salad dressing or mayonnaise
½ cup grated Parmesan cheese

Toasted bread crumbs
Wheat Chips or Rye Chips, page 10, crackers or crisp vegetable relishes

Makes about 2 cups

Cut each artichoke into sixths. In small mixing bowl or microwave-proof serving dish, combine artichokes, salad dressing and cheese. Microwave at High 3 to 4 minutes, or until hot, stirring carefully after 2 minutes and at the end. Sprinkle with crumbs. Serve hot with chips, crackers or vegetables.

Rye Chips

½ cup all-purpose flour
½ cup rye flour
½ teaspoon salt
1 teaspoon caraway seed, optional
¼ cup plus 2 tablespoons butter or margarine
3 to 4 tablespoons cold water

Makes 3½ dozen

Photo directions below.

Wheat Chips

1 cup whole wheat flour
½ teaspoon salt
1 to 3 teaspoons sesame or other seed, optional
¼ cup plus 2 tablespoons butter or margarine
3 to 4 tablespoons cold water

Makes 3½ dozen

Cheese Stix

1 cup all-purpose flour
½ teaspoon salt
2 teaspoons caraway or dill seed, optional
1 cup shredded colby or Cheddar cheese
⅓ cup shortening
¼ cup water
3 or 4 drops yellow food coloring

Makes about 3½ dozen

In mixing bowl, combine flour, salt, seed and cheese. Cut in shortening at low speed or with pastry blender until particles are fine. Combine water and food coloring. Sprinkle over mixture while stirring with fork, until dough is just moist enough to hold together.

Form into square. Flatten to ½-in. thickness. Roll out on floured pastry cloth to 15×9-in. rectangle; smooth or trim edges. Sprinkle lightly with salt. Cut into 3×1-in. sticks. Arrange, close together, in a ring around edge of lightly greased microwave-proof baking sheet or large pie plate.

Microwave at High 3 to 5 minutes, or until dry and puffy, rotating ½ turn after 2 minutes. Watch closely. Remove immediately from sheet with metal spatula.

How to Microwave Rye Chips & Wheat Chips

Combine flour(s), salt and seed in mixing bowl. Cut in butter at low speed or with pastry blender until particles are coarse.

Sprinkle water over mixture while stirring with fork, until dough is just moist enough to hold together.

Form into square. Flatten to ½-in. thickness. Roll out on floured pastry cloth to 14×12-in. rectangle; smooth or trim edges. Cut into 2-in. squares.

Arrange, close together, in a ring around edge of lightly greased microwave-proof baking sheet or large pie plate. Place 1 to 3 in center.

Microwave at High 2 to 6 minutes, or until dry and firm to touch; rotate ½ turn after 1 minute. If microwaving less than 6; allow 20 to 30 seconds per chip.

Remove to wire rack carefully. (Chips will crisp as they stand.) Serve as a cracker or with a chip dip.

10

Wheat Chip Nachos

1 recipe Wheat Chips dough,
   opposite
2 cups (8-oz.) shredded
   Cheddar or Monterey Jack
   cheese (or a combination)
½ teaspoon chili powder

Makes 18 to 24

Prepare dough for Wheat Chips. Divide into thirds. Form each into ball; flatten to ½-in. thickness. Roll out on floured pastry cloth to 8-in. circle. Place each on lightly greased baking sheet or large pie plate. Prick with fork to mark into 6 or 8 wedges.

Microwave, one at a time, at High 2 to 4 minutes, or until dry and firm to touch, rotating ½ turn after 1 minute. Remove carefully to wire rack or wax paper.

At serving time, combine cheese and chili powder. Place rounds on wax paper on microwave plate. Sprinkle each with ⅔ cup of the cheese. Microwave at 50% (Medium) 1 to 2 minutes, or until cheese is melted, rotating ¼ turn every 20 seconds. Cut into wedges. Serve immediately.

NOTE: Rounds may be topped with sliced hot peppers, olives or cooked sausage before sprinkling with cheese.

Olive Snack Nuggets

1 recipe Basic Biscuit Dough,*
   page 19
⅓ cup dry bread crumbs
2 tablespoons grated
   Parmesan cheese
½ teaspoon chili powder
36 stuffed small olives, well
   drained
¼ cup butter or margarine,
   melted

Makes 36 appetizers

Roll or pat out dough to 6-in. square; cut into 1-in. squares. In mixing bowl combine crumbs, cheese and chili powder. Wrap each dough piece around olive; pinch to seal. Coat with butter, then crumb mixture. Place in 1-qt. microwave-proof ring mold or 9-in. pie plate which has a buttered glass, open-end up, in center.

Microwave at High 3 to 5 minutes, or until nuggets spring back when touched lightly in several places, rotating ½ turn after half the time. Remove glass. Serve warm.

*1 can refrigerator biscuits may be substituted. Quarter each biscuit and wrap around olive.

11

Deep-Dish Pizza Nibblers

1 teaspoon dry yeast
3 tablespoons warm water
¼ cup warm milk
1 tablespoon sugar
2 tablespoons butter or margarine, melted
½ teaspoon salt
3 or 4 drops yellow food coloring
1¼ to 1½ cups all-purpose flour
½ cup dry bread crumbs
1 tablespoon poppy seed
2 tablespoons butter or margarine, melted

Makes two 9-in. pizzas

Pizza Topping

12 ounces seasoned lean pork sausage
1 medium-small onion, chopped (½ cup)
¼ green pepper, chopped
1 tablespoon chopped fresh parsley or parsley flakes
½ teaspoon oregano
¼ teaspoon garlic powder or 1 small clove garlic, minced
1 can (8 oz.) tomato sauce
1 can (6 oz.) tomato paste
2 cups (8 oz.) shredded mozzarella cheese
Parsley and grated Parmesan cheese, optional

Variations:

Pepperoni Pizza: Place 3½-ozs. sliced pepperoni on several layers of paper towels; cover with paper towel. Microwave at High 25 seconds to 1 minute. Place pepperoni on top of pizza before sprinkling with cheese.

Mushroom Pizza: Substitute 1 pound sliced fresh mushrooms for sausage. Microwave in 2 tablespoons butter with onion, 3 to 4 minutes. Salt and pepper mixture to taste and add ¼ teaspoon basil.

How to Microwave Deep-Dish Pizza Nibblers

Combine yeast and water in mixing bowl. Stir in milk, sugar, butter, salt and food coloring. Gradually stir in flour until stiff.

Knead about 1 minute, or until smooth; form into ball. Place in greased bowl. Cover; let rise until light and doubled in size, in microwave oven, page 38 or about 1 hour in warm place.

Microwave one at a time at 50% (Medium) 4 to 6 minutes, or until dry and springs back when touched lightly in several places, rotating ½ turn every 2 minutes.

Place crumbled sausage and onion in 2-qt. casserole. Microwave at High 4 to 6 minutes, or until sausage is cooked, stirring every 2 minutes. Drain off fat.

Combine crumbs and poppy seed. Brush two 9-in. pie plates generously with butter. Sprinkle each with 1 tablespoon crumbs. Roll out dough, ½ at a time, on floured surface to 10-in. circle.

Fit into pie plate, pressing up sides as necessary; do not cover rim. Brush dough generously with butter, then sprinkle with remaining crumb mixture, coating entire shell.

Cover; let rise at room temperature 30 minutes or in microwave oven through 1 process. Prick bottom several places with fork. If shell has slipped down side, press into place.

Stir in green pepper, seasonings, tomato sauce and paste. Microwave at High 5 to 6 minutes, or until boiling and cooked, stirring every 2 minutes.

Spread half the mixture in each of the bread shells. Sprinkle with mozzarella (1 cup per pie), parsley and Parmesan cheese.

Microwave, one pie at a time, at High 5 to 7 minutes, or until cheese is melted and hot in the middle; rotate ½ turn after half the time. Let stand 5 to 10 minutes.

Breads

Breads & Browning

Most breads can be micro-waved. The exceptions are breads which require a very hard crust, and pancakes, waffles, doughnuts and popovers. All of them can be warmed in the microwave oven.

Microwaved breads do not brown. For an attractive appearance, they should be made with naturally colorful ingredients or given one of the toppings suggested here.

There are two types of bread, yeast and quick. Those made with yeast need time to rise. Most quick breads are leavened with baking powder or soda and can be mixed and baked immediately.

Follow the measuring and mixing techniques on page 4.

Compare a plain microwaved biscuit with one which was baked conventionally and a third which was coated with bread crumbs before microwaving.

Save leftover bread, coffee-cake, cake, cookies, cereal, snack chips, or crackers to make crumbs for toppings.

Toppings for Breads, Rolls & Biscuits

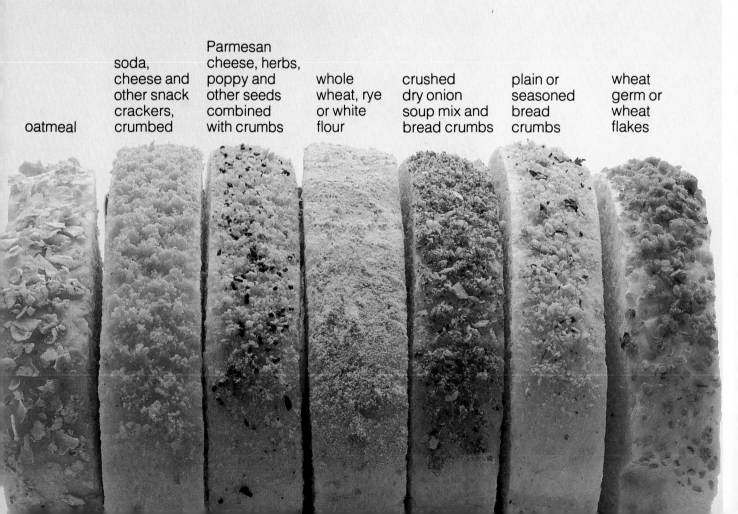

oatmeal

soda, cheese and other snack crackers, crumbed

Parmesan cheese, herbs, poppy and other seeds combined with crumbs

whole wheat, rye or white flour

crushed dry onion soup mix and bread crumbs

plain or seasoned bread crumbs

wheat germ or wheat flakes

Sprinkle 1 teaspoon of crumbs on the top of each muffin or 3 to 4 tablespoons on a coffeecake. Add additional crumbs near end of microwaving, if desired.

Coat breads or 10 to 12 rolls or biscuits with melted butter before rolling in bread crumbs or flour.

Brush with milk when coating bread or rolls with wheat germ, oatmeal, crushed cereal, cracker or other coarse crumbs.

Toppings for Coffeecakes, Sweet Rolls, Muffins & Cupcakes

cinnamon sugar

cake or muffins dried & crumbed

cookies crumbed

graham cracker crumb

graham cracker crumbs with cinnamon sugar

Streusel Topping: mix ½ cup flour, 2 to 4 tablespoons white or brown sugar, cinnamon, 2 tablespoons butter

sweet rolls and coffeecake pieces dried and crumbled

Breads: Quick

Biscuits

Biscuits should always be served hot. A plate of hot microwaved biscuits can be ready for the table in less than 5 minutes, about half the time it takes to preheat a conventional oven, and they can be baked and served in the same dish.

A homemade mix makes biscuits even easier. The mix keeps up to 4 to 5 weeks in the refrigerator and several months in the freezer. It can also be used for quick muffins and coffeecakes.

Make-ahead Mix

10 cups all-purpose flour,
   divided
 6 tablespoons baking powder
 1 tablespoon salt
1½ cups butter, margarine or
   shortening, cut in small
   pieces

Makes 13 cups mix

How to Prepare Make-ahead Mix

Use 5 or 6-qt. mixing bowl. Combine half the flour with all the baking powder and salt.

Cut in butter with low speed of mixer or pastry blender until particles are fine. Add remaining flour and mix until well combined.

Place in container with tight cover. Label, date and refrigerate or freeze for later use.

Basic Biscuits

1 cup Make-ahead Mix,
    opposite
¼ to ⅓ cup milk
2 tablespoons butter or
    margarine, melted
⅓ cup dry bread crumbs

Makes 9 (2-in.) biscuits

Variations:

Cheese Biscuits: Combine ½ cup shredded Cheddar cheese with the mix before adding milk. (Half cheese and half crisp, crumbled, microwaved bacon is a good combination.)

Bacon Caraway Biscuits: Combine ⅓ cup crisp, crumbled microwaved bacon (3 or 4 strips) and ½ teaspoon caraway seed, optional, with the mix before adding milk.

How to Microwave Basic Biscuits

Combine Make-ahead Mix and milk in mixing bowl. Stir only until dough clings together. If sticky, add 1 or 2 tablespoons mix.

Knead dough on floured surface about 10 times for lightness, flakiness and height.

Roll or pat out to ½-in. thickness. Cut straight down with 2-in. cutter, or pat out to 6-in. square; cut into 2-in. square biscuits.

Brush with butter, then sprinkle with crumbs. You may add 1 teaspoon herbs, poppy or caraway seed, or use half grated Parmesan cheese.

Place close together in a ring around edge of large pie plate, shallow baking dish or microwave-proof baking sheet.

Microwave at High 2 to 4 minutes, or until dry and puffy, rotating ½ turn every minute. Remove to wire rack immediately. Serve warm.

19

Shortcake Biscuits

1½ cups Make-ahead Mix,
    page 18
  2 tablespoons sugar
  1 egg, beaten
  3 tablespoons milk
  2 tablespoons butter or
    margarine, melted
 ¼ cup graham cracker or
    cookie crumbs
    Fruit and whipped cream

Makes 6 to 8 servings

In mixing bowl, combine Make-ahead Mix, sugar, egg and milk. Stir only until dry particles are moistened. If sticky, add 1 or 2 tablespoons mix. Knead on floured surface 10 times. Roll out or pat to ½-in. thickness (no thinner). Cut into 2¼-in. rounds with floured cutter. Coat with butter, then crumbs. Place close together around edge of 10-in. pie plate or large microwave-proof plate. (If necessary, micro-wave half the biscuits at a time.)

Microwave 2 to 3½ minutes, or until biscuit springs back when touched, and is no longer doughy on inside, rotating ½ turn after half the time. Remove to paper towel or wire rack. Serve warm. Split, fill and top with fruit and whipped cream.

Cinnamon Ring

2 cups Make-ahead Mix,
  page 18
⅔ cup milk
½ cup sugar
¼ cup graham cracker crumbs
2 teaspoons cinnamon
¼ cup finely chopped nuts or
  flaked or shredded
  coconut, optional
¼ cup butter or margarine,
  melted
  Vanilla Icing, page 92

  Makes 1 coffee cake (20 rolls)

In mixing bowl, combine Make-ahead Mix and milk just until dough forms. If sticky, add 1 or 2 tablespoons mix. Knead on floured surface 10 times. Combine sugar, crumbs, cinnamon and nuts. Roll out or pat to ¼- to ½-in. thickness. Cut into 2-in. rounds with floured cutter. Coat with butter, then sugar mixture. Stand rounds in 1-qt. ring mold or arrange around edge of pie dish or large plate; overlap rounds.

Microwave at High 4 to 7 minutes, or until top springs back when touched in several places, rotating ½ turn after half the time. Cool 2 minutes; loosen and turn out onto serving plate. Frost with Vanilla Icing while warm.

Jam Dandy Breakfast Cake

¼ cup graham cracker or
  cookie crumbs, divided
1 cup Make-ahead Mix,
  page 18
¼ cup sugar
2 tablespoons butter or
  margarine, melted
⅓ cup milk
1 egg, beaten
  Jam or marmalade

  Makes 9-in. coffeecake

Butter 9-in. pie plate or dinner plate. Place buttered glass, open-end up, in center. Sprinkle with about 1 tablespoon crumbs. In small mixing bowl, combine Make-ahead Mix, sugar, butter, milk and egg. Stir in only until dry ingredients are moistened. Drop by spoonfuls around edge of plate. Sprinkle with remaining crumbs. Drop ½ teaspoon jam in center of each spoonful of batter.

Microwave at High 2½ to 4½ minutes, or until cake springs back when touched lightly in several places, rotating ½ turn after half the time. Remove glass. Serve warm.

Baking Powder Biscuit Dough

You can substitute this dough for Make-ahead Mix and the milk in Shortcake Biscuits, opposite. To make Cinnamon Ring, opposite, double the recipe below.

1 cup all-purpose flour
1½ teaspoons baking powder
¼ teaspoon salt
2 tablespoons shortening,
  butter or margarine
⅓ cup plus 1 tablespoon milk

  Makes 9 (2-in.) biscuits

In mixing bowl, combine flour, baking powder and salt. Cut in shortening until particles are fine. Add milk; stir only until dough clings together.

How to Make Jam Dandy

Drop spoonfuls of batter around edge of plate. Sprinkle with crumbs. Drop jam in center of each spoonful of batter.

Dinner Breads

Dinner breads accompany a meal. Sausage Corn Bread can be served as an inexpensive main dish. To make traditional corn bread, omit the sausage.

Sausage Corn Bread

 1 pound bulk pork sausage
¾ cup all-purpose flour
¾ cup yellow cornmeal
 1 tablespoon sugar
 1 tablespoon baking powder
½ teaspoon salt
 2 eggs, beaten
½ cup milk
⅓ cup sausage drippings,
    melted shortening or
    cooking oil

Makes 9-in. round loaf

Variation:

Cheese 'n Corn Bread:
Substitute 1½ cups shredded Cheddar cheese and 1 teaspoon chili powder for sausage. Stir into corn bread batter.

NOTE: The variation does not need to be set on an inverted saucer during microwaving.

How to Microwave Sausage Corn Bread

Crumble sausage over bottom of 9-in. round baking dish. Microwave at High 4½ to 7 minutes, stirring after half the time. Drain off fat, reserving ⅓ cup for the corn bread. Reserve half the sausage in another dish.

Combine remaining ingredients in mixing bowl. Stir only until smooth. Pour over sausage in baking dish. Crumble reserved sausage over top. Center dish on inverted saucer in oven. Microwave at 50% (Medium) 6 minutes, rotating ¼ turn every 3 minutes.

Increase power to High. Microwave 2 to 6 minutes, rotating every 2 minutes. Check for doneness by looking through bottom of clear glass dish. No unbaked batter should appear in center. Let stand 10 minutes before removing from dish. Serve warm.

Savory Cheese Bread

  2 cups all-purpose flour
  1 tablespoon dry onion flakes
  2 teaspoons poppy seed
  2 teaspoons sugar
1½ teaspoons baking powder
  ½ teaspoon soda
  ½ teaspoon salt
  ½ cup shredded Cheddar
      cheese
  ¼ cup plus 2 tablespoons
      butter or margarine
  ⅔ cup buttermilk or sour milk*
  1 egg, slightly beaten

Topping:
  1 teaspoon butter or
      margarine, melted
  2 tablespoons dry bread
      crumbs
  2 tablespoons grated
      Parmesan cheese
  1 teaspoon poppy seed

    Makes 10- or 9-in. round loaf

Combine topping ingredients
until crumbly.

*To sour milk, combine 1
tablespoon lemon juice or
vinegar with enough milk to
measure ⅔ cup.

How to Microwave Savory Cheese Bread

Combine in mixing bowl, flour, onion flakes, poppy seed, sugar, baking powder, soda, salt and cheese. Cut in butter at low speed of mixer or with pastry blender until particles are fine. Stir in buttermilk and egg until well blended.

Turn into 10-in. pie plate or 9-in. round baking dish which has been lightly greased, then lined with wax paper. Shape into rounded loaf with spoon. Sprinkle with topping. Make several ½-in. deep crisscross cuts across top with sharp knife.

Microwave at 50% (Medium) 6 minutes, rotating ½ turn every 3 minutes. Increase power to High. Microwave 3 to 6 minutes, or until no longer doughy in center, rotating ½ turn every 2 minutes. Let stand 10 minutes. Serve slightly warm or cold, cut into thin wedges or slices.

Quick Bread Loaves

Except for corn bread, most quick bread loaves are baked in loaf dishes and served in thin slices. They keep fresh for several days when stored in an air tight plastic bag or foil in the refrigerator rather than at room temperature. They also freeze well in loaves or serving size portions.

How to Microwave Quick Breads

Chop nuts or cut fruit finely. Microwave batters become thinner so large pieces will sink.

Select the deeper 8×4- or 9×5-in. dish with straight sides. Avoid the shallow meat loaf dish.

Line bottom of dish with strip of wax paper. Spread batter in dish. Shield ends of loaf with 2-in. wide strips of foil.

Place loaf on inverted saucer in oven. Microwave at 50% (Medium), rotating dish ¼ turn every 3 minutes.

Remove foil shields. Increase power to High. Microwave 2 to 8 minutes as directed in recipe.

Look through bottom of dish. Bread is done when no unbaked batter appears in center bottom, which is the last place to cook.

Avoid overcooking, which usually occurs on inside of loaf where it is not visible.

Let bread stand in dish on countertop 10 minutes. Loosen edges and turn out on rack.

Remove wax paper. Cool completely before cutting into thin slices for serving.

24

Pumpkin Nut Bread

1 cup all-purpose flour
¾ cup sugar (half packed
    brown, if desired)
1 teaspoon baking powder
1 teaspoon soda
1 teaspoon salt
2 teaspoons pumpkin pie spice
    or cinnamon
½ cup cooking oil
2 eggs
½ cup chopped nuts, optional
1 cup cooked or canned
    pumpkin

Makes 8×4- or 9×5-in. loaf

Blend ingredients in mixing bowl at low speed 15 seconds; beat at medium speed 1 minute.

Spread batter in 8×4- or 9×5-in. loaf dish lined on bottom with wax paper. Shield ends of loaf with 2-in. wide strips of foil, covering 1-in. batter and molding remainder around handles.

Center loaf dish on inverted saucer in oven. Microwave at 50% (Medium) 9 minutes, rotating ¼ turn every 3 minutes. Remove foil. Increase power to High. Microwave 2 to 5 minutes. If using clear glass dish, check for doneness by looking through bottom. No unbaked batter should appear in center. Let stand 5 to 10 minutes before removing from dish.

Variations:

Carrot Nut Bread: Substitute 1½ cups shredded carrots for the pumpkin.

Zucchini Bread: Substitute 1½ cups shredded, unpared zucchini for the pumpkin.

Applesauce Bread: Substitute 1 cup sweetened applesauce for the pumpkin.

Nut Bread: Mix 1 tablespoon lemon juice and enough milk to make ½ cup; substitute for pumpkin. Increase nuts to 1 cup.

NOTE: If there is a slight bubble over the top in the 8×4-in. dish, next time make a few cupcakes.

Whole Wheat ► Banana Bread

1 cup whole wheat flour
½ cup all-purpose flour
¾ cup sugar (½ cup packed
    brown sugar, if desired)
½ cup, plus 2 tablespoons
    butter or margarine,
    room temperature
⅓ cup milk
2 eggs
2 very ripe medium bananas,
    sliced
1 tablespoon lemon juice or
    vinegar
1 teaspoon soda
½ teaspoon salt
½ cup chopped nuts, if desired
1 recipe Streusel Topping,
    page 17

Makes 8×4- or 9×5-in. loaf

NOTE: Bread may be baked in a 6-cup or large ring dish. Line bottom with wax paper, or grease.

Variations:

Basic Banana Bread: Subtitute white flour for whole wheat flour.

Holiday Banana Bread: Stir 1 cup mixed candied fruit into batter after beating. Microwave at High 1 to 3 minutes longer.

How to Microwave Whole Wheat Banana Bread

Place all ingredients except topping in large mixing bowl in order given. Blend at low speed 15 seconds; beat at medium speed 2 minutes.

Spread batter in 8×4- or 9×5-in. loaf dish lined on bottom with wax paper; sprinkle with topping. Shield ends of loaf with 2-in. wide strips of foil, covering 1-in. of batter and molding remainder around handles of dish.

Center loaf dish on inverted saucer in oven. Microwave at 50% (Medium) 9 minutes; rotate ¼ turn every 3 minutes. Increase power to High. Microwave 4 to 7½ minutes; remove foil after 2 minutes and rotate every 2 minutes.

◄ Cracker Brown Bread

¾ cup all-purpose flour
¾ cup graham cracker crumbs
1 teaspoon soda
½ teaspoon salt
½ cup raisins
¾ cup buttermilk or sour milk*
¼ cup molasses
¼ cup melted shortening or
    cooking oil

Makes 2 round loaves

Blend ingredients in mixing bowl. Line bottom of 2-cup measure with circle of wax paper. Pour in half the batter. Cover with vented plastic wrap.

Microwave at 50% (Medium) 5½ to 7 minutes, or until top springs back when touched lightly and no unbaked batter appears on side, rotating ½ turn every 3 minutes. Cool 5 to 10 minutes before removing from measure. Microwave second loaf.

Serve warm. Reheat slices on plate. Cover loosely with plastic wrap. Microwave at High 30 to 60 seconds.

*To sour milk, combine 1 tablespoon lemon juice or vinegar with enough milk to measure ¾ cup.

Country Raisin Loaf ▲

1 cup raisins
1 cup water
1 tablespoon grated orange
    peel, optional
½ cup sugar
⅓ cup shortening
2 eggs

2 teaspoons baking powder
1 teaspoon cinnamon
½ teaspoon soda
½ teaspoon salt
¼ teaspoon nutmeg
    Dash cloves
1⅓ cups all-purpose flour

Makes 8×4- or 9×5-in. loaf

In mixing bowl, combine raisins and water. Microwave at High 3 minutes. Stir in peel; cool. Combine remaining ingredients except flour in mixing bowl; beat until blended. Blend in flour, then the raisin mixture.

Spread batter in 8×4- or 9×5-in. loaf baking dish lined on bottom with wax paper. Shield ends of loaf with 2-in. wide strips of foil, covering 1 in. of batter and molding remainder around handles of dish.

Center loaf dish on inverted saucer in oven. Microwave at 50% (Medium) 9 minutes, rotating ¼ turn every 3 minutes. Remove foil. Increase power to High. Microwave 2 to 6 minutes, or until done. Let stand 10 minutes before removing from dish.

Check for doneness by looking through bottom of clear glass dish. No unbaked batter should appear in center. Let stand on countertop 5 to 10 minutes before removing from dish.

27

◀ Applesauce Spice Loaf

 1⅓ cups all-purpose flour
 ¾ cup sugar
 1 teaspoon soda
 1 teaspoon salt
 1 teaspoon cinnamon
 ¼ teaspoon nutmeg
 ¼ teaspoon cloves
 ¼ cup shortening
 ¾ cup sweetened applesauce
 ½ cup chopped raisins or nuts
 2 eggs
 ¼ cup milk
 2 teaspoons vinegar or lemon
  juice

  Makes 8×4- or 9×5-in. loaf

Blend ingredients in large mixing bowl at low speed 15 seconds; beat at medium speed 2 minutes.

Spread batter in 8×4- or 9×5-in. loaf dish lined on bottom with wax paper. Shield ends of loaf with 2-in. wide strips of foil, covering 1-in. of batter and molding remainder around handles of dish.

Center loaf dish on inverted saucer in oven. Microwave at 50% (Medium) 9 minutes, rotating ¼ turn every 3 minutes.

Increase power to High. Microwave 3 to 5 minutes, removing foil after 2 minutes and rotating every 2 minutes.

If using clear glass dish, check for doneness by looking through bottom. No unbaked batter should appear in center. Let stand 5 to 10 minutes before removing from dish.

NOTE: If quick bread loaves should be uncooked in center, return to dish. Set on inverted saucer in oven. Microwave at High 1 to 2 minutes.

Date Nut Bread ▲

1 cup dates, halved	¼ cup shortening
1 teaspoon soda	1 egg
¾ cup boiling water	1½ cups all-purpose flour
¾ cup packed brown or	1 teaspoon salt
granulated sugar	½ cup chopped nuts
1 tablespoon grated orange	
peel, optional	Makes 8×4- or 9×5-in. loaf

In mixing bowl, combine dates, soda and water. Let stand about 10 minutes. Mix sugar, peel, shortening and egg. Blend in date mixture, then flour, salt and nuts.

Spread batter in 8×4- or 9×5-in. loaf baking dish lined on bottom with wax paper. Shield ends of loaf with 2-in. wide strips of foil, covering 1 in. of batter and molding remainder around handles of dish.

Center loaf dish on inverted saucer in oven. Microwave at 50% (Medium) 8 minutes, rotating ¼ turn every 2 minutes. Remove foil. Increase power to High. Microwave 2 to 6 minutes. If using clear glass dish, check for doneness by looking through bottom. No unbaked batter should appear in center. Let stand 5 to 10 minutes before removing from dish.

Muffins

Muffins are the quickest of all breads to microwave. One muffin can be ready in less than 1 minute. Since muffins are best warm, microwave at serving time.

Many batters, especially those leavened with soda, will keep in the refrigerator a few days. The Ready-to-go Mix can be kept 6 to 8 weeks, so you can mix ahead and bake as needed.

Make up muffin batter and have on hand in the refrigerator. In less than a minute, you can have a hot muffin for breakfast or lunch.

Muffin Chart

High Power	
1 muffin	20-40 seconds
2 muffins	½-1½ minutes
4 muffins	1-2½ minutes
6 muffins	2½-4½ minutes

How to Microwave Muffins

Line each custard cup or microwave cupcake dish with two paper liners. When microwaving only 3 or 4 muffins in the cupcake dish, alternate cups for even baking.

Place all muffin ingredients in bowl. Mix quickly and lightly only until particles are moistened.

Fill cups half full. Cups of microwave dishes are small, so don't overfill. Sprinkle with topping.

Arrange in ring when microwaving 3 or more muffins at a time. Rotate and rearrange after half the time.

Remove from cups to wire rack immediately after baking. (Moist spots will dry on standing.)

Follow photo directions and time chart on page 29.

Mexican Corn Muffins

½ cup all-purpose flour
½ cup yellow cornmeal
½ cup drained canned or frozen (thawed) whole kernel corn
¼ cup chopped green pepper
1 tablespoon sugar
2 teaspoons baking powder
½ teaspoon salt
½ teaspoon chili powder
⅓ cup milk (part corn liquid may be used)
1 egg, slightly beaten
¼ cup cooking oil or melted shortening

Makes 8 to 10 medium muffins

Whole Wheat Muffins

1 cup whole wheat flour
¼ cup molasses
2 tablespoons brown sugar
1½ teaspoons baking powder
1 teaspoon anise or fennel seed, optional
½ teaspoon salt
⅓ cup milk
¼ cup cooking oil or melted shortening
1 egg
¼ cup raisins, optional

Makes 8 to 10 medium muffins

Luncheon Muffins

1 cup all-purpose flour
1 tablespoon sugar
1½ teaspoons baking powder
½ teaspoon paprika
¼ teaspoon salt
½ cup shredded Cheddar cheese
2 slices bacon, microwaved and crumbled
2 tablespoons chopped green pepper
2 tablespoons finely chopped onion
½ cup milk
¼ cup cooking oil or melted butter or margarine
1 egg

Makes 10 to 12 medium muffins

Ready-to-go Honey Bran Muffins

2 cups boiling water
6 cups 100% all-bran or bran
    flakes, divided
1 cup honey
2 cups sugar (half packed
    brown sugar, if desired)
1 cup shortening
1 tablespoon, plus 2 teaspoons
    soda
2 teaspoons salt
4 eggs
5 cups all-purpose flour, divided
4 cups buttermilk

Makes 8 to 9 dozen
medium muffins

Variation:

Ready-to-go Molasses Oatmeal Muffins: Increase water to 2½ cups and substitute molasses for honey. Substitute quick-cooking rolled oats for 4 cups bran.

NOTE: Raisins, nuts, dates or other fruits may be added at the time the muffins are microwaved.

How to Make Ready-to-go Honey Bran Muffins

Combine water, 2 cups bran and honey in mixing bowl. Set aside. In 5- or 6-qt. mixing bowl, mix sugar, shortening, soda and salt. Add eggs; beat well.

Stir in half the flour. Blend in buttermilk, then remaining flour. Add soaked bran and remaining 4 cups bran; blend well.

Pour batter into large plastic bowl, ice cream pail or coffee cans. Cover tightly, date and refrigerate and use as directed. To microwave follow directions on page 29.

Coffeecakes

Quick bread coffeecakes are similar to dessert cakes in texture, but are slightly less rich and sweet. While they are not frost-ed, they usually have a topping which gives them an appealing appearance without special browning techniques. Follow the directions on page 4 for measuring and mixing ingredients.

How to Microwave Coffeecakes

Place all ingredients except topping in mixing bowl. Beat at low speed until well blended, about 30 seconds.

Spread batter in 8-in. square dish or dish recommended in recipe. Cover with topping. Shield corners of square dish with foil triangles.

Microwave at 50% (Medium) 6 minutes, rotating ¼ turn every 2 minutes. (If recipe directs, place dish on inverted saucer.) Remove foil from square dish.

Increase power to High. Microwave 2 to 6 minutes, rotating dish ¼ turn each time you check for doneness.

Check through bottom of glass dish; only small amount of unbaked batter should appear in center. Top should be almost dry and spring back when touched.

Let dish stand directly on counter top 10 minutes to complete cooking.

Spice Kuchen

1½ cups all-purpose flour
¾ cup sugar
1 teaspoon baking powder
1 teaspoon cinnamon
½ teaspoon soda
½ teaspoon salt
¼ teaspoon nutmeg
¼ teaspoon cloves
¾ cup buttermilk or sour milk*
½ cup margarine or
    shortening, melted
1 egg, beaten

Topping:

⅓ cup packed brown sugar
¼ cup all-purpose flour
½ cup chopped nuts
½ teaspoon cinnamon
2 tablespoons butter or
    margarine, melted

Makes 8-in. square coffeecake

See photo directions opposite for mixing cake.

Combine topping ingredients until crumbly.

*To sour milk combine 1 tablespoon lemon juice or vinegar with enough milk to measure ¾ cup.

Cranberry Crisscross Cake

1¼ cups all-purpose flour
½ cup sugar
⅓ cup shortening
1¼ teaspoons baking powder
½ teaspoon salt
1 egg
½ cup milk
1 pkg. (11 oz.) cranberry relish
    (1½ cups)
¼ cup cinnamon sugar*

Makes 9-in. round coffeecake

In mixing bowl, blend flour, sugar, shortening, baking powder, salt, egg and milk; beat at low speed 1 minute.

*To make cinnamon sugar, combine ¼ cup sugar and 1 teaspoon cinnamon.

How to Microwave Cranberry Crisscross Cake

Spread half the batter in 9-in. round baking dish. Top with half the cranberry relish. Cover with remaining batter. Spoon remaining relish on top in strips to make a lattice top. Sprinkle with cinnamon sugar.

Center dish on inverted saucer in oven. Microwave at 50% (Medium) 6 minutes, rotating dish ¼ turn every 3 minutes. Increase power to High. Microwave 4 to 7 minutes, or until cake springs back when touched lightly in center.

Breads: Yeast

Yeast is a living organism which feeds on sugar for growth. It produces leavening gas bubbles which make dough rise and give bread its porous structure.

The most commonly used yeast is the dry form. For the best results use it before the expiration date printed on the back of the packet.

Kneading develops a good structure in the bread. It blends ingredients and stretches the gluten into a fine elastic framework which holds yeast gas bubbles. Wheat flour, which produces gluten, is necessary for making good bread.

Rising or proofing is an important part of yeast cell development. Use the microwave oven to shorten the time needed for rising. Bread which is to be baked in a conventional oven can be proofed in a microwave oven if you use a container which is suitable to both.

Baking sets the gluten and brings out the flavor of bread. When bread is placed in the oven, a quick-rising period takes place. This rising, called "oven spring" continues until the heat which kills yeast action has reached the entire loaf.

Storage. Microwaved breads are moister on the surface than conventionally baked, and do not keep as long. Use the bread in 2 or 3 days. Bread may also be cut into serving portions and frozen the first day. Freezing does not improve the product, but will maintain the quality for several months.

Microwaved yeast doughs require special formulation. The recipe for white dough below can be shaped into loaves, rolls or coffeecakes.

Basic Rich Dough

  1 packet active dry yeast
  ¼ cup warm water
  ½ cup warm milk
  1 egg
  2 tablespoons sugar
  1 teaspoon salt
  ¼ cup butter or margarine, melted
  8 to 10 drops yellow food coloring, optional
2½ to 3 cups all-purpose flour

Follow photo directions on page 36.

Microwave Yeast Bread Tips

Dark breads are attractive when coated with a topping before microwaving. (See ideas on page 16.) Because of expansion during rising, white breads should be heavily coated with dark crumbs for a brown crust.

Make your own ring dish, if you don't have one, by placing a greased glass, open-end up, in the center of a 3-qt. casserole.

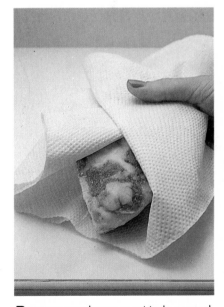

Rewarm only amount to be used. Wrap in napkin or paper towel. For coffeecake or loaf, start with 30 seconds at High, rotate after half the time. Add 10 to 15 seconds at a time, if necessary.

How to Prepare Basic Rich Dough

Soften dry yeast in water which feels slightly warm (120°). Cold temperatures retard growth of yeast cells; too much heat will kill yeast action.

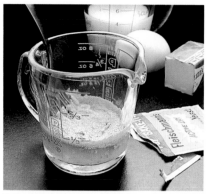

Stir dry yeast to help soften and dissolve instantly. In large bowl, combine yeast with remaining ingredients except flour; beat well.

Add flour gradually to form a very stiff dough, beating well after each addition to distribute yeast and other ingredients evenly throughout the dough.

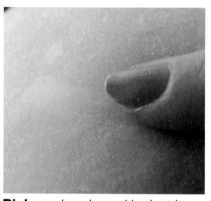

Pick up dough, and look at it closely. Tightly stretch it and you will see tiny bubbles under the satiny surface.

Form kneaded dough into a smooth ball; place in greased bowl. Turn ball over to coat all sides. This helps prevent crusting of surface during rising.

Cover; let rise until light and doubled in size in microwave, page 38, or 1 to 1½ hours in warm place. Surface will be stretched and light with bubbles.

How to Microwave Basic Rich Dough

Grease or butter deep dishes lightly. If bread is covered with crumbs, shallow dishes or plates need not be greased.

Dense batters do not cook completely through on the bottom unless the dish is placed on an inverted saucer.

Microwave loaves at 50% (Medium) 6 minutes, then at High 3 to 6 minutes. Microwave small breads at 50% entire time.

Knead on well-floured surface; folding half the dough over on itself toward you. Push with palms. Turn dough one quarter turn. Repeat process rhythmically.

Sprinkle kneading surface with more flour if dough sticks. As kneading progresses, dough loses its stickiness and becomes smooth and satiny.

Test for adequate kneading after 5 minutes by holding the dough in your hand for about 15 seconds; it should not stick to your hand.

Test dough by pressing 2 fingers about 1-in. into it. If impressions remain, the dough is risen sufficiently. Punch down dough, let rest 5 to 10 minutes.

Shape and coat dough and let rise as directed in recipes on the following pages. Cover dough with wax paper when rising in microwave, use plastic wrap when rising at room temperature.

Judge shaped dough by appearance only. If shaped bread rises too much, gluten strands become weak; bread may collapse while baking. Underrisen dough produces a small, heavy bread.

Rotate all bread products every 2 to 3 minutes for even rising and cooking. This is especially important in an oblong or square dish.

Touch bread lightly in several places. (Test ring shapes on top, inside and outside.) If done, it will spring back. Overcooking toughens bread.

Let stand in dish a couple minutes to continue cooking. Then loosen and turn out onto rack or serving plate. Cool thoroughly before storing.

How to Rise Dough in the Microwave Oven

Place dough in well greased microwave-proof bowl, large enough to hold it when doubled. Turn to coat dough with fat.

Set bowl in dish of hot water; cover loosely with wax paper. (If dough will touch paper, dust inside with flour.)

Microwave, following chart below, for 1 to 4 minutes. Let stand 15 minutes. Rotate bowl of water ¼ turn.

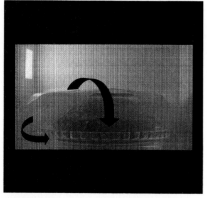

Turn dough over in bowl carefully if surface appears to be drying. Repeat microwaving, standing and rotating cycle until dough is light and doubled in size.

Punch down dough and shape as directed in your recipe.

Power Level and Time Chart

Half or more of rising time can be saved by microwaving. Select one of the following settings to rise dough in the microwave oven. Use the lower setting if your oven has an uneven pattern.

50% — Microwave 1 minute, let stand 15 minutes.

30% — Microwave 1 minute, let stand 15 minutes.

10% — Microwave 4 minutes, let stand 15 minutes.

How to Rise Shaped Dough in the Microwave Oven

Place shaped dough in microwave-proof dish. If it is to be baked in conventional oven, dish must also be tolerant to oven temperatures.

Set in or on top of dish of hot water. Tent with wax paper floured on inside. If recipe makes two loaves, rise and cook one in the microwave while the other is rising at room temperature.

Repeat the microwaving, standing and rotating cycle following chart above, until dough rises to volume described in recipe. Remove water and wax paper before cooking.

Basic Loaf

1 recipe Basic Rich Dough,
   page 35
1/3 cup fine dry bread crumbs
1 tablespoon grated Parmesan
   cheese
1 teaspoon poppy seed
2 tablespoons butter or
   margarine, melted

Makes 1 loaf

Let dough rise and rest as
directed on page 36. Combine
crumbs, cheese and poppy
seeds. Brush loaf with butter
then coat with crumb mixture.
Place in greased 8×10-in. loaf
dish. Let rise until light and
doubled in size, in microwave
oven, opposite, or about 1 hour
in warm place.

Place dish on inverted saucer in
microwave oven. Microwave at
50% (Medium) 6 minutes,
rotating 1/4 turn every 3 minutes.
Increase power to High.
Microwave 30 seconds to 2 minutes, or until top springs back
when touched lightly in several
places, rotating 1/4 turn every minute. Let stand 5 minutes. Remove
bread; cool on wire rack.

Bubble Dinner Bread

1 recipe Basic Rich Dough,
   page 35
1 envelope dry onion soup or
   1/4 cup grated Parmesan
   cheese

Crunchy Finger Rolls

1 recipe Basic Rich Dough,
   page 35
2/3 cup dry bread crumbs
2 tablespoons grated
   Parmesan cheese
1 tablespoon poppy seed
1/4 cup butter or margarine,
   melted

Makes 20 rolls

Let dough rise and rest as
directed on page 36. Combine
crumbs, cheese and poppy
seed. Divide dough into 20
pieces. Shape each into 4-in.
strip. Coat with butter, then
crumb mixture. Arrange 10
strips crosswise in each of 2
well-greased 8×4-in. loaf
dishes. Cover; let rise until light
and doubled in size, in
microwave oven, opposite, or
about 1 hour in warm place.
Sprinkle with any remaining
crumb mixture.

Microwave 1 loaf dish at a time at
50% (Medium) 3½ to 8 minutes,
or until tops spring back when
touched lightly in several places,
rotating 1/4 turn every 1½ to 2
minutes. Let stand 2 minutes.
Remove rolls; cool on wire rack.

1/4 cup dry bread crumbs
36 small stuffed olives or 1/2-in.
   cheese or ham cubes
1/4 cup butter or margarine,
   melted

Makes 1 loaf

Let dough rise and rest as directed on page 36. Crumb dry onion
soup in blender or food processor; combine with bread crumbs.
Divide dough into 36 pieces. Shape each piece around olive. Coat
with butter, then crumbs. Layer in lightly greased 10- or 12-cup
microwave bundt or tube dish.* Cover; let rise until light and doubled
in size, in microwave oven, opposite, or 1 to 1½ hours in warm place.

Microwave at 50% (Medium) 6 minutes, rotating 1/4 turn every 3
minutes. Increase power to High. Microwave 30 seconds to 5
minutes, or until top springs back when touched lightly in several
places, rotating 1/4 turn every 2 minutes. Let stand 2 minutes. Loosen
edges and turn out onto serving plate.

*A 2½-qt. round casserole may be used. Place greased glass,
open-end up, in center.

Cheese Whirls

1 recipe Basic Rich Dough, page 35, risen and rested, page 36
1 cup shredded Cheddar cheese, divided
¾ cup cheese cracker crumbs, divided
½ cup dry bread crumbs
¼ cup butter or margarine, melted

Makes 20 rolls

Variation:

Cheese Swirl Loaf: Prepare rolls as directed below. Layer, let rise and microwave as directed for Cinnamon Loaf (opposite).

How to Microwave Cheese Whirls

Divide dough in half and roll each into 10-in. square on lightly floured surface.

Sprinkle each square with ½ cup cheese and 2 tablespoons cracker crumbs. Combine remaining cracker crumbs and bread crumbs. Roll up squares. Cut each into ten 1-in. slices. Roll in butter, then coat with crumbs.

Place 10 rolls, cut-side down, in circle about 1-in. from edge of large plate or in 10-in. pie plate. Repeat with remaining rolls.

Cover; let rise until light and doubled in size in microwave oven, page 38, or about 1 hour in warm place. Sprinkle with remaining crumbs.

Microwave 1 plate at a time at 50% (Medium) 4 to 8 minutes, or until tops spring back when touched lightly in several places, rotating ¼ turn every 2 minutes.

Daisy Cinnamon Loaf

1 recipe Basic Rich Dough, page 35, risen and rested, page 36
¼ cup sugar
1 cup graham cracker crumbs, divided
2 teaspoons cinnamon
¼ cup plus 2 tablespoons butter or margarine, melted
    Vanilla Icing, page 92

Makes 1 loaf

Variation:

Daisy Cinnamon Rolls:
Prepare rolls as directed below. Arrange, let rise and microwave as directed for Cheese Whirls (opposite). Top each hot roll with 1 tablespoon jam. Drizzle with icing while warm.

How to Microwave Daisy Cinnamon Loaf

Combine sugar, ¼ cup crumbs and cinnamon. Divide dough in half and roll each into 10-in. square on lightly floured surface. Brush each square with 1 tablespoon butter; sprinkle each with half the sugar mixture. Roll up squares. Cut each square into ten 1-in. slices. Roll slices in remaining butter, then coat with remaining crumbs.

Layer rolls, cut-side down, in lightly greased 10- or 12-cup bundt or tube dish or 3-qt. round casserole with greased glass, open-end up, in center.

Cover; let rise until light and doubled in size in microwave oven, page 38, or about 1 hour in warm place. Sprinkle with remaining crumbs.

Microwave at 50% (Medium) 6 minutes, rotating ¼ turn every 3 minutes. Increase power to High. Microwave 30 seconds to 6 minutes or until tops spring back when touched lightly in several places. Let stand 2 minutes. Loosen edges and turn out onto serving plate. Drizzle with icing while warm.

Apple Monkey Bread

1 recipe Basic Rich Dough,
  page 35, risen and rested,
  page 36
⅓ cup granulated sugar
⅓ cup packed brown sugar
⅓ cup graham cracker or
  cookie crumbs
2 teaspoons cinnamon
3 tablespoons butter or
  margarine, melted
2 medium apples, pared and
  each cut into 12 slices

Makes 1 coffeecake

How to Microwave Apple Monkey Bread

Combine sugars, crumbs and cinnamon. Divide dough into 24 pieces.Coat with butter, then sugar mixture.

Layer in buttered 10- or 12-cup microwave-proof bundt or cake dish, arranging apple slice next to each dough piece.

Cover; let rise until light and doubled in size in microwave oven, page 38, or about 1 hour in warm place. Sprinkle with any remaining sugar mixture.

Microwave at 50% (Medium) 6 minutes, rotating ¼ turn every 3 minutes. Increase power to High.

Microwave 30 seconds to 6 minutes, or until top springs back when touched lightly in several places, rotating ¼ turn every 2 minutes.

Let stand 2 minutes. Loosen edges of bread and turn out onto serving plate.

Streusel Coffeecake

1 recipe Basic Rich Dough,
     page 35, risen and rested,
     page 36
¼ cup granulated sugar
¼ cup packed brown sugar
¾ cup all-purpose flour
1 teaspoon cinnamon
¼ cup butter or margarine,
     room temperature
     Vanilla Icing, page 92

Makes 2 coffeecakes

Variation:

Apple Streusel: Arrange 2 apples, pared and thinly sliced, on coffeecake before sprinkling with sugar mixture.

How to Microwave Streusel Coffeecake

Combine sugars, flour, cinnamon and butter at low speed or with pastry blender until particles are fine.

Press dough into 2 well-greased 9-in. round baking dishes or 9- or 10-in. pie plates. Sprinkle with sugar mixture.

Cover; let rise until light and doubled in size in microwave oven, page 38, or about 1 hour in warm place.

Place dish on inverted saucer in microwave oven. Microwave 1 dish at a time at 50% (Medium) 5 to 9 minutes, or until top springs back when touched lightly, rotating ¼ turn every 3 minutes.

Let stand 5 minutes. Drizzle with icing while warm.

Heidelberg Pumpernickel Round

1 packet active dry yeast
½ cup warm water
1 cup mashed potatoes, room temperature
½ cup dark or black strap molasses
¼ cup shortening, melted
1 teaspoon caraway seed
1 teaspoon salt
1 cup rye flour
1 to 1½ cups all-purpose flour
1 cup plus 3 tablespoons whole wheat flour, divided
3 tablespoons cornmeal
1 tablespoon butter or margarine, melted

Makes 1 loaf

How to Microwave Heidelberg Pumpernickel Rye

Combine yeast and water in large mixing bowl. Stir in potatoes, molasses, shortening, caraway seed and salt.

Stir in rye, all-purpose and 1 cup whole wheat flour gradually to form a very stiff dough.

Knead on well-floured surface about 8 minutes, or until smooth. Place in greased bowl; cover.

Shape dough into 15-in. strip. Brush with butter; coat well with remaining flour-cornmeal mixture.

Form strip into ring in pie plate. Pinch ends together. Place greased glass, open-end up, in center of plate.

Cover; let rise until light, in microwave oven, page 38, or about 1 hour in warm place (dough may not double in size).

44

Let rise until almost doubled in size in microwave oven, page 38, or about 1½ hours in warm place.

Punch down dough. Shape into ball. Cover with bowl; let rest 15 minutes. Combine 3 tablespoons whole wheat flour and cornmeal. Sprinkle some over well-greased 10-in. pie plate or microwave-proof baking sheet.

Microwave at 50% (Medium) 6 minutes, rotating ¼ turn every 3 minutes. Increase power to High. Microwave 2 to 7 minutes, rotating ¼ turn every 2 minutes.

Test by touching lightly in several places; top should spring back. Let stand 10 minutes. Remove bread to wire rack.

Swedish Rye Bread

1 cup rye flour
⅓ cup dark or black strap
  molasses
¼ cup shortening
1 teaspoon salt
¾ cup boiling water
1 packet active dry yeast
¼ cup warm water
½ cup raisins, optional
2 to 2½ cups all-purpose flour
  Wheat germ or cornmeal
  Milk

Makes 1 loaf

Variation:

Swedish Rye Bread Loaf:
Punch down dough; let rest 10
minutes. Shape into loaf. Brush
with milk, then coat with wheat
germ. Place in well-greased
8×4-in. loaf dish. Let rise as
directed. Place loaf dish on
inverted saucer in microwave
oven; microwave as directed.

To shape loaf: Roll out on lightly
floured surface to 15×6-in. rectangle. Roll up tightly starting with
6-in. end. Seal ends and bottom.

How to Microwave Swedish Rye Bread

Combine rye flour, molasses,
shortening, salt and boiling
water in large mixing bowl. Cool
to warm. Combine yeast and
warm water. Stir yeast and
raisins into rye flour mixture. Stir
in all-purpose flour gradually to
form a very stiff dough.

Knead on well-floured surface
about 8 minutes, or until smooth.
Place in greased bowl; cover.
Let rise until light and doubled in
size in microwave oven, page 38,
or 1 to 1½ hours in warm place.
Punch down; shape into ball. Cover with bowl; let rest 10 minutes.

Sprinkle well-greased 10-in. pie
plate or microwave-proof baking
sheet with wheat germ. Shape
dough into 15-in. strip. Brush
with milk; coat well with additional wheat germ. Shape into ring in
pie plate. Pinch ends together.

◄Butter Crumb Rye Rolls

1 recipe Swedish Rye Bread
  Dough, opposite
½ cup dry bread crumbs
½ teaspoon each oregano, basil
  and marjoram
¼ cup butter or margarine,
  melted

Makes 24 rolls

Combine crumbs and herbs.
Divide dough into 24 pieces.
Shape into balls. Coat with
butter, then crumbs. Place 9 rolls
around edge and 3 rolls in
center of each of 2 well-greased
10-in. pie plates or baking
dishes. Cover; let rise until light
and doubled in size, in
microwave oven, page 38, or 1
to 1½ hours in warm place.

Microwave 1 plate at a time at
50% (Medium) 6 to 8 minutes, or
until tops spring back when
touched lightly, rotating ¼ turn
every 1½ to 2 minutes. Let stand
5 minutes. Remove rolls; cool on
wire rack.

Place greased glass, open-end
up, in center. Cover; let rise until
light and doubled in size in
microwave oven, page 38, or in
warm place.

Microwave at 50% (Medium) 6
minutes, rotating ¼ turn every 3
minutes. Increase power to High.
Microwave 2½ to 6 minutes,
rotating ¼ turn every 2 minutes.

Test by touching lightly in
several places, top will spring
back when done. Let stand 10
minutes. Remove bread; cool on
wire rack.

Cakes

With a microwave oven, you can have fresh, homemade cake whenever you want. Make the size that's right for you. There's no preheating, and no wasted energy if you bake one layer instead of two.

Cake Dishes. The cakes in this book can be microwaved in several different dish sizes and shapes. The recipes provide quantities for both one and two layers. We suggest clear glass or plastic to help you check the bottom of the cake for doneness.

Ingredients. Shortening, butter and margarine are not interchangeable in cakes. Do not make substitutions. If you wish to use cake flour rather than all purpose flour, increase the amount by 2 to 3 tablespoons for each cup of flour. It is usually safe to substitute flavoring ingredients, if you desire.

Browning. Microwave cakes do not brown. Once the cake is frosted, this difference is not apparent. However, the top can also be soft and sticky. To dry the top and make it easier to frost, sprinkle about 1 tablespoon graham cracker crumbs on each layer after baking.

How to Choose the Right Microwave Dish

One-layer recipe will make a 9-in. round, 8×8- or 10×6-in. cake, or 14 to 16 cupcakes.

Two-layer recipe will make two 9-in. round, 8×8- or 10×6-in. cakes, or 12×8-in. cake plus 4 to 8 cupcakes.

Ring or Bundt cakes are made from two-layer recipes in a 12- or 14-cup tube pan. If using 12-cup pan make 2 or 3 cupcakes.

How to Prepare Dishes

Layer cakes. For single layer cakes to be frosted and served from dish, no preparation is needed. For two-layer cakes, line bottoms with two circles of wax paper for easy removal. A few dabs of grease under paper will keep it from slipping when batter is spread.

Plain or fluted bundt cake. Grease dish well and coat with graham cracker crumbs. Shake out excess crumbs.

How to Mix Cakes and Fill Dishes

Place all cake ingredients in mixing bowl. Blend on lowest speed until dry particles are moistened. This prevents spatters when speed is increased.

Beat at medium or "cake" speed 2 minutes. With a hand mixer, use one of the higher speeds.

Scrape side of bowl occasionally while mixing. With a standard mixer, hold rubber spatula against side of bowl as it turns.

Clean beaters with spatula and stir this mixture into batter thoroughly. Any unblended batter will sink and make a hole in the bottom of the cake.

Spread batter in dishes, filling no more than ⅓ to ½ full. With a 12×8-in. dish, make 4 to 8 cupcakes. Some cakes make very full 9-in. round or 10×6-in. layers, so bake 2 to 4 cupcakes if necessary. For bundt cake, use a 14-cup dish.

How to Turn Out Cakes

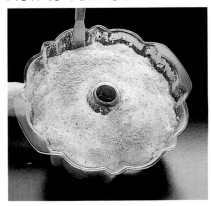  

Loosen edges with flexible spatula. Loosen every flute and around the tube of bundt dish. Lift cake from bottom.

Top dish with wire rack; invert dish. If cake does not unmold, loosen edges again. Do not force cake out of dish.

Cut cakes served from pan with sharp knife. Remove pieces with small, flexible pancake turner. After the first piece, the rest will come out easily.

How to Microwave Cakes

Place dish in oven, set 12×8-in. dish on inverted saucer. Microwave at 50% (Medium) following chart below. Rotate dish ¼ turn every 3 minutes.

Increase power to High. Microwave until cake tests done, rotating dish ½ turn every time you check for doneness.

Let stand directly on counter top. If a few moist spots appear on top, they will dry as cake cools.

Cake Microwaving Chart

Cake Shape	Comments	Microwave at 50% (Medium)	Microwave at High	Let Stand On Countertop
Single Layer 9-in. round 8-in. square 10×6-in.	Use 1-layer recipe. Some recipes make very full layers, so bake 1 or 2 cupcakes	6 minutes	2 to 6 min.	until cool serve from dish
12×8-in. plus 4 to 8 cupcakes	Use 2-layer recipe. Set dish on inverted saucer in oven	9 minutes	2 to 8 min.	until cool serve from dish
Two Layer 9-in. round 8-in. square (2) 10×6-in. (2)	Use 2-layer recipe Microwave I layer at a time	6 minutes	2 to 6 min.	5 to 10 min.
Ring or Bundt 14 cup size 12 cup size, plus 3 to 6 cupcakes	Use 2-layer recipe.	12 minutes	2 to 8 min.	10 to 15 min.
Cupcakes 14 to 16 cupcakes	Use 1-layer recipe.	see chart on page 62		Remove to wire rack immediately

52

How to Test for Doneness

Look at top of cake. Most of it should appear cooked. A few moist spots will evaporate as cake cools.

Touch top lightly in several places. It should spring back. Many cakes just start to pull away from sides of dish.

Microwave cake longer if center starts to sink as cake is removed from the oven. Set on inverted saucer if bottom is unbaked.

Check through bottom of glass dish. If a 2- to 3-in. area in center appears unbaked, it will cook as cake stands on countertop.

No unbaked batter should appear on bottom of tube or loaf cakes. They are too deep to bake done during standing time.

Sprinkle top with graham cracker crumbs so it won't be sticky. Cool layer and tube cakes 10 to 15 minutes on countertop before removing from dishes.

Devils Food Cake

One-layer cake:
¾ cup all-purpose flour
⅔ cup sugar
½ teaspoon soda
½ teaspoon salt
½ teaspoon vanilla
 1 ounce pre-melted
　　unsweetened chocolate*
⅓ cup shortening
⅓ cup milk
 2 eggs

Two-layer cake:
1¾ cups all-purpose flour
1⅓ cups sugar
 ¾ teaspoon soda
 1 teaspoon salt
 1 teaspoon vanilla
 2 ounces pre-melted
　　unsweetened chocolate*
⅔ cup shortening
¾ cup milk
 4 eggs

Place all ingredients except 1 (2) egg(s) in mixing bowl. Blend at low speed, then beat at medium speed 1 minute. Add remaining egg(s); beat 1 minute. See page 50 for dish preparation. Spread batter in one or two 9-in. round, 8×8- or 10x6-in. baking dish(es).

Microwave 1 layer at a time at 50% (Medium) 5 to 6 minutes, rotating ¼ turn every 3 minutes. Increase power to High. Microwave 2 to 5 minutes, or until done. Let stand directly on countertop 5 to 10 minutes.

*If solid chocolate is used, melt as directed on page 7. Add to batter while mixing.

Variations:

Chocolate Mint Cake: Substitute peppermint flavoring for vanilla.

Chocolate Peanut Cake: Add 2 tablespoons (¼ cup) peanut butter and 1 (2) more tablespoons milk before mixing.

Chocolate Cherry Cake: Add 2 tablespoons (¼ cup) maraschino cherry juice for milk and ¼ cup (½ cup) cut-up maraschino cherries before mixing.

Chocolate Mallow Cake

One-layer cake:	**Two-layer cake:**
⅔ cup all-purpose flour	1⅓ cups all-purpose flour
⅔ cup sugar	1⅓ cups sugar
¾ teaspoon soda	1½ teaspoons soda
½ teaspoon salt	1 teaspoon salt
½ teaspoon vanilla	1 teaspoon vanilla
¼ cup shortening	½ cup shortening
2 eggs	4 eggs
1 ounce unsweetened chocolate, pre-melted or solid, melted	2 ounces unsweetened chocolate, pre-melted or solid, melted
2 tablespoons water	⅓ cup water
½ cup dairy sour cream	1 cup dairy sour cream
10 to 12 regular marshmallows, cut in half	20 to 24 regular marshmallows, cut in half

Place all ingredients, except marshmallows, in mixing bowl. Blend at lowest speed, then beat at medium speed 2 minutes. Spread batter in one or two 9-in. round, 8×8- or 10×6-in. baking dish(es).*

Microwave at 50% (Medium) 6 minutes. Rotate ¼ turn every 3 minutes. Increase power to High. Microwave 2 to 5 minutes, or until done. Let stand directly on countertop 5 to 10 minutes.

To frost, follow photo directions below.

*When using 9-in. round and 10×6-in. pan, make 2 to 4 cupcakes.

How to Frost Chocolate Mallow Cake

Place marshmallows, cut side down and close together, on cake after it has stood 3 to 4 minutes. Cool cake and frost with Chocolate Frosting, page 70.

Cut between marshmallows. Cake slices more easily if allowed to stand several hours after frosting.

Old-fashioned Oatmeal Cake

One-layer cake:
½ cup quick-cooking oats
½ cup boiling water
¾ cup all-purpose flour
½ cup sugar
⅓ cup packed brown sugar
½ teaspoon soda
½ teaspoon salt
½ teaspoon cinnamon
¼ teaspoon baking powder
¼ teaspoon nutmeg
⅓ cup shortening
2 eggs
3 tablespoons water
¼ cup chopped nuts

Two-layer cake:
1 cup quick-cooking oats
1 cup boiling water
1½ cups all-purpose flour
1 cup sugar
⅔ cup packed brown sugar
1 teaspoon soda
1 teaspoon salt
1 teaspoon cinnamon
½ teaspoon baking powder
½ teaspoon nutmeg
⅔ cup shortening
4 eggs
⅓ cup water
½ cup chopped nuts

Combine oats and boiling water; set aside. Combine remaining ingredients in mixing bowl. Blend at low speed, then beat at medium speed 2 minutes. Beat in oats mixture at low speed 20 to 30 seconds. See page 50 for dish preparation. Spread batter in one or two 9-in. round, 8×8- or 10×6-in. baking dish(es).

Place dish on inverted saucer in microwave oven. Microwave 1 layer at a time at 50% (Medium) 5 to 6 minutes, rotating ¼ turn every 3 minutes. Increase power to High. Microwave 2 to 6 minutes, or until done. Let stand directly on countertop 5 to 10 minutes. Meanwhile, prepare Caramel Topping, below.

Caramel Topping:
¼ cup butter or margarine
2 tablespoons cream

1 cup packed brown sugar
½ cup chopped nuts or coconut

How to Microwave Caramel Topping

Combine butter and cream in small mixing bowl. Microwave at 50% (Medium) 1¼ to 3 minutes, or until butter is melted. Stir in brown sugar and nuts.

Spread carefully on warm layers. Microwave 1 layer at a time at High 2 to 3 minutes, or until topping bubbles in a few spots.

Applesauce Cake

One-layer cake:
 1 cup all-purpose flour
⅔ cup sugar
 1 teaspoon soda
½ teaspoon salt
½ teaspoon cinnamon
¼ teaspoon nutmeg
¼ teaspoon cloves
⅓ cup shortening
½ cup applesauce
 2 eggs
 3 tablespoons milk
¼ cup chopped nuts or
    raisins, optional

Two-layer cake:
 2 cups all-purpose flour
1¼ cups sugar
1½ teaspoons soda
 1 teaspoon salt
 1 teaspoon cinnamon
½ teaspoon nutmeg
¼ teaspoon cloves
⅔ cup shortening
 1 cup applesauce
 4 eggs
⅓ cup milk
½ cup chopped nuts or
    raisins, optional

Place all ingredients in mixing bowl. Blend at low speed, then beat at medium speed 2 minutes. See page 50 for dish preparation. Spread batter in one or two 9-in. round, 8×8- or 10×6-in. baking dish(es).

Microwave 1 layer at a time at 50% (Medium) 6 minutes, rotating ¼ turn every 3 minutes. Increase power to High. Microwave 2 to 5 minutes, or until done. Let stand directly on countertop 5 to 10 minutes.

Banana Nut Cake

One-layer cake:
 1 cup all-purpose flour
⅔ cup sugar
½ teaspoon soda
½ teaspoon salt
½ teaspoon vanilla
⅓ cup shortening
 2 eggs
 3 tablespoons milk*
 2 teaspoons lemon juice or
    vinegar
 1 very ripe medium banana,
    thinly sliced
¼ cup finely chopped nuts,
    optional

Two-layer cake:
 2 cups all-purpose flour
1¼ cups sugar
 1 teaspoon soda
 1 teaspoon salt
 1 teaspoon vanilla
⅔ cup shortening
 4 eggs
⅓ cup milk*
 1 tablespoon lemon juice or
    vinegar
 2 very ripe medium bananas,
    thinly sliced
½ cup finely chopped nuts,
    optional

Place all ingredients in mixing bowl. Blend at low speed, then beat at medium speed 2 minutes. See page 50 for dish preparation. Spread batter in one or two 9-in. round, 8×8- or 10×6-in. baking dish(es).

Microwave 1 layer at a time at 50% (Medium) 6 minutes, rotating ¼ turn every 3 minutes. Increase power to High. Microwave 2 to 6 minutes, or until done. Let stand directly on countertop 5 to 10 minutes.

*Buttermilk may be substituted for milk and lemon juice.

◄ Carrot Cake

One-layer cake:	**Two-layer cake:**
¾ cup all-purpose flour	1½ cups all-purpose flour
¾ cup sugar	1½ cups sugar
1 teaspoon baking powder	1½ teaspoons baking powder
½ teaspoon soda	1 teaspoon soda
1 teaspoon cinnamon	2 teaspoons cinnamon
¼ teaspoon nutmeg	¼ teaspoon nutmeg
½ cup cooking oil	1 cup cooking oil
1 cup finely shredded carrots	2 cups finely shredded carrots
2 eggs	4 eggs
¼ cup finely chopped nuts	½ cup finely chopped nuts

Place all ingredients in mixing bowl. Blend at low speed, then beat at medium speed 2 minutes. See page 50 for dish preparation. Spread batter in one or two 9-in. round, 8×8- or 10×6-in. baking dish(es).

Microwave 1 layer at a time at 50% (Medium) 6 minutes, rotating ¼ turn every 3 minutes. Increase power to High. Microwave 2 to 6 minutes, or until done. Let stand directly on countertop 5 to 10 minutes. Cool and frost with Cream Cheese Frosting, below.

Cream Cheese Frosting:*

2 tablespoons butter or margarine	½ pkg. (4-oz. size) cream cheese, room temperature
1 tablespoon cream	2½ to 3 cups confectioners' sugar

In mixing bowl, combine butter, cream and cream cheese. Microwave at 50% (Medium) about 1 minute, or until warm. Blend well. Beat in sugar until of spreading consistency. If necessary, thin with a few drops cream.

*For one-layer cake, use half the recipe.

58

◄ Date Nut Cake

One-layer cake:
½ cup dates, quartered
⅓ cup boiling water
½ teaspoon soda
⅓ cup shortening
⅔ cup sugar
2 eggs
1 cup all-purpose flour
½ teaspoon salt
¼ cup chopped nuts

Two-layer cake:
1 cup dates, quartered
⅔ cup boiling water
1 teaspoon soda
⅔ cup shortening
1¼ cups sugar
4 eggs
1¾ cups all-purpose flour
1 teaspoon salt
½ cup chopped nuts

Combine dates, water and soda; set aside. Beat shortening and sugar 2 minutes. Add date mixture and remaining ingredients. Blend at low speed, then beat at medium speed 2 minutes. See page 50 for dish preparation. Spread batter in one or two 9-in. round, 8×8- or 10×6-in. baking dish(es).

Microwave 1 layer at a time at 50% (Medium) 6 minutes, rotating ¼ turn every 3 minutes. Increase power to High. Microwave 2 to 5 minutes, or until done. Let stand directly on countertop 5 to 10 minutes.

Pumpkin Cake

One-layer cake:
1 cup all-purpose flour
¾ cup packed brown sugar
½ cup cooked or canned
   pumpkin
½ teaspoon soda
½ teaspoon salt
½ teaspoon cinnamon
¼ teaspoon baking powder
¼ teaspoon ginger
¼ teaspoon nutmeg
⅛ teaspoon cloves
⅓ cup shortening
3 tablespoons milk
2 eggs

Two-layer cake:
2 cups all-purpose flour
1½ cups packed brown sugar
1 cup cooked or canned
   pumpkin
1 teaspoon soda
1 teaspoon salt
1 teaspoon cinnamon
½ teaspoon baking powder
½ teaspoon ginger
¼ teaspoon nutmeg
¼ teaspoon cloves
⅔ cup shortening
⅓ cup milk
4 eggs

Place all ingredients in mixing bowl. Blend at low speed, then beat at medium speed 2 minutes. See page 50 for dish preparation. Spread batter in one or two 9-in. round, 8×8- or 10×6-in. baking dish(es).

Microwave 1 layer at a time at 50% (Medium) 6 minutes, rotating ¼ turn every 3 minutes. Increase power to High. Microwave 2 to 5 minutes, or until done. Let stand directly on countertop 5 to 10 minutes.

Short-Cut Idea: Substitute 1 (2) teaspoon(s) pumpkin pie spice for spices in recipe.

NOTE: Cake may be topped with whipped cream and Sour Cream Sauce, page 147, if desired.

◄ Whole-Egg Yellow Cake

One-layer cake:
  1 cup all-purpose flour
  ⅔ cup sugar
  1¼ teaspoons baking powder
  ½ teaspoon salt
  ½ teaspoon vanilla
  ⅓ cup shortening
  2 eggs
  ⅓ cup milk
  2 teaspoons grated orange
    peel, optional

Two-layer cake:
  2 cups all-purpose flour
  1¼ cups sugar
  2½ teaspoons baking powder
  1 teaspoon salt
  1 teaspoon vanilla
  ⅔ cup shortening
  4 eggs
  ¾ cup milk
  1 tablespoon grated orange
    peel, optional

Place all ingredients in mixing bowl. Blend at low speed, then beat at medium speed 2 minutes. See page 50 for dish preparation. Spread batter in one or two 9-in. round, 8×8- or 10×6-in. baking dish(es).

Microwave 1 layer at a time at 50% (Medium) 6 minutes, rotating ¼ turn every 3 minutes. Increase power to High. Microwave 1 to 5 minutes, or until done. Let stand directly on countertop 5 to 10 minutes.

NOTE: For bundt cake, decrease baking powder to 2 teaspoons and use 14-cup or larger tube dish.

Variation: ►

Poppy Seed Cake: Add 2 tablespoons (¼ cup) poppy seed to milk. Mix and microwave as directed.

◄ White Cake

One-layer cake:
  1 cup cake flour*
  ⅔ cup sugar
  1½ teaspoons baking powder
  ½ teaspoon salt
  ½ teaspoon vanilla or almond
    extract
  ⅓ cup shortening
  ¼ cup milk
  1 egg
  2 egg whites (¼ cup)

Two-layer cake:
  2 cups cake flour*
  1⅓ cups sugar
  3 teaspoons baking powder
  1 teaspoon salt
  1 teaspoon vanilla or almond
    extract
  ⅔ cup shortening
  ½ cup milk
  2 eggs
  4 egg whites (½ cup)

Place all ingredients in mixing bowl. Blend at low speed, then beat at medium speed 2 minutes. See page 50 for dish preparation. Spread batter in one or two 9-in. round, 8×8- or 10×6-in. baking dish(es).

Microwave 1 layer at a time at 50% (Medium) 6 minutes, rotating ¼ turn every 3 minutes. Increase power to High. Microwave 2 to 5 minutes, or until done. Immediately sprinkle with graham cracker crumbs, if desired. Let stand directly on countertop 5 to 10 minutes.

*If all-purpose flour is used, increase milk to ⅓ (⅔) cup.

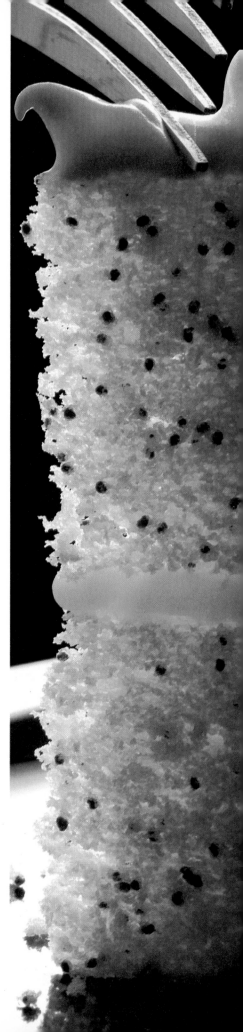

Cupcakes

Cupcakes are extremely easy and quick to microwave. You can make one in about half a minute. For fresh cupcakes daily, store batter in the refrigerator and use as needed. The one layer size cake recipe will make 14 to 16 cupcakes. Soda leavened batters can be refrigerated up to a week, and baking powder batters 3 to 4 days. No special pans are needed; cupcake liners and custard cups will do. Use two paper liners in each cup to absorb moisture during baking.

Cupcakes rise higher when microwaved, so use less batter than you would for conventional baking. For most batters, one third full is the right amount. Microwave a sample cupcake to test the amount of rising. Microwave muffin dishes have smaller cups, so use less batter in the liners than you do for custard cups.

Cupcake Chart

Quantity	High Power
1	25 to 30 seconds
2	¾ to 1¼ minutes
3*	1 to 1½ minutes
4*	1½ to 2 minutes
6*	2 to 3 minutes

*Rotate and rearrange after half the time.

How to Microwave Cupcakes

Place two paper cupcake liners in each 5 or 6 oz. custard cup or in microwave muffin dishes.

Fill each about ⅓ full. An old-fashioned ice cream scoop makes a good measure. Use less batter in muffin dishes.

Cut through batter with wooden pick to prevent large air spaces which can form because cupcakes bake quickly.

Arrange in ring in oven. Microwave at High, following chart. Rearrange or rotate after half the time as chart indicates.

Microwave until almost dry on top. Small moist spots will dry on standing. Overmicrowaving makes dry and tough cupcakes.

Remove cupcakes from cups as soon as they are microwaved. Let stand on wire cooling rack.

Gingerbread Cupcakes

 1 cup all-purpose flour
½ cup sugar
½ teaspoon soda
½ teaspoon salt
½ teaspoon ginger
¼ teaspoon nutmeg
¼ teaspoon cinnamon
⅛ teaspoon cloves
 2 eggs
⅓ cup shortening
¼ cup light molasses
¼ cup boiling water

Makes 12 to 16 cupcakes

Place all ingredients in mixing bowl. Blend at low speed, then beat at medium speed 2 minutes. Make cupcakes as directed, opposite. Frost while warm with Orange Frosting, page 69.

Variation:

Ginger Cake: Spread batter in 9-in. round, 8×8- or 10×6-in. baking dish. Microwave at 50% (Medium) 5 to 6 minutes, rotating ¼ turn every 3 minutes. Increase power to High. Microwave 2 to 6 minutes, or until done. Cool and frost, serve warm or cold.

Peanut Butter Cups

 1 cup all-purpose flour
¾ cup packed brown sugar
 1 teaspoon baking powder
½ teaspoon salt
½ teaspoon vanilla
¼ cup shortening
 3 tablespoons peanut butter
 2 eggs
½ cup milk

Makes 15 to 18 cupcakes

Place all ingredients in small mixing bowl. Blend at low speed, then beat at medium speed 2 minutes. Make cupcakes as directed, opposite. Frost while warm with Peanut Butter Frosting page 69.

Southern Jam Cake

1½ cups all-purpose flour
⅔ cup sugar
½ teaspoon soda
½ teaspoon salt
1 teaspoon cinnamon
¼ teaspoon cloves
¼ teaspoon nutmeg
⅔ cup shortening
½ cup fruit preserves, jam or
   marmalade (cherry, plum,
   apricot or orange)
4 eggs
⅓ cup milk
1 tablespoon lemon juice
½ cup finely chopped nuts

Makes 1 tube or bundt cake

Place all ingredients in mixing bowl. Blend at low speed, then beat at medium speed 2 minutes.

Follow photo directions below.

Variation:

Dark Fruitcake: Coat 1 cup broken nuts, 2 cups mixed candied fruit and 2 to 3 cups raisins (part cut-up dates, if desired) with ¼ cup all-purpose flour. Stir into batter. Turn batter into prepared 12-cup tube dish. When cool, wrap tightly and store at least 8 hours before slicing.

How to Microwave Southern Jam & Pound Cakes

Grease 10- or 12-cup bundt or tube dish well. Coat with graham cracker crumbs. Spread batter in dish.

Place greased glass, open-end up, in 2½- to 3-qt. casserole before filling with batter. (For fruitcake, a clear bowl is preferable.) Line flat bottom tube dish or 9×5- or 8×4-in. loaf dish with wax paper and omit greasing, if desired. (If using 8×4-in. dish make 4 to 6 cupcakes.)

Pound Cake

1 cup butter or margarine at room temperature
1 cup sugar
4 eggs
1 teaspoon vanilla
1½ cups all-purpose flour
½ teaspoon baking powder
½ teaspoon salt

Makes 1 tube or bundt cake

Cream butter and sugar until fluffy. Add remaining ingredients. Blend at low speed 1 minute.

Follow photo directions below.

Variations:

Lemon or Orange Pound Cake: Add 2 to 3 teaspoons grated lemon or orange peel.

Butter Pecan Pound Cake: Melt 2 tablespoons butter or margarine in small bowl at High. Stir in ½ cup finely chopped pecans. Microwave 2 minutes, stirring after 1 minute. Cool; add with flour.

Light Fruit Cake: Stir 1 to 2 cups chopped nuts, 1 to 2 cups white or dark raisins and 2 cups mixed candied fruit into batter. When cool, wrap tightly and store at least 8 hours before slicing.

Shape 2-in. strip of foil around handles and covering 1-in. of batter if using a loaf dish.

Microwave at 50% (Medium) 8 minutes for Pound Cakes and 12 minutes for Jam and Fruit Cakes, rotating ¼ turn every 3 minutes. Remove foil from loaf dish. Increase power to High.

Microwave 1 to 6 minutes (4 to 10 minutes for fruitcakes), or until done. No unbaked batter should appear on bottom of loaf dish. Cool directly on countertop 10 minutes. Turn out on wire rack.

Frostings

More than one frosting will complement the flavor of each type of cake, so be creative. Frostings pictured, left to right; top row: Chocolate Mallow, Buttercream, Maple; second row: Lemon, Butterscotch, Orange; third row: Peanut Butter, Chocolate, Browned Butter; bottom row: Coffee, Cherry Nut, Butter Pecan.

How to Microwave Frosting

Combine liquid and butter in mixing bowl. Microwave until bubbling for a good cooked frosting flavor.

Add confectioners' sugar and flavorings. Beat until smooth and of spreading consistency.

Make frosting stiff enough to hold deep swirls, but soft enough to look moist.

Thin frosting by adding a few drops of liquid at a time. Warm frosting may need thinning as it cools while you are using it.

Add additional confectioners' sugar if the frosting is too soft or thin to hold its shape. Leftover frosting can be refrigerated.

Soften refrigerated frosting by microwaving at High 20 to 30 seconds. Add a few drops milk if necessary.

How to Frost Cakes

Freeze very tender cakes for easier frosting. Thinly frost sides of cake to set crumbs; repeat with heavier coat.

Save about ½ cup of frosting for top of cake. Frost in 2 steps as directed for sides.

Make swirls, using small metal spatula or back of a teaspoon. A sprinkle of coconut or nuts can be used to decorate frosting.

Butter Pecan Frosting

3 tablespoons butter or
   margarine
¼ cup finely chopped pecans
1 to 2 tablespoons cream or milk
2 cups confectioners' sugar
½ teaspoon vanilla

> Frosts tops of 2 layers,
> 12×8-in. cake or
> 2½ doz. cupcakes

Microwave butter in small mixing bowl at High 1 minute, or until melted. Stir in pecans. Microwave at High 2 to 4 minutes, or until browned, stirring after 2 minutes. Add remaining ingredients. Beat until smooth and of spreading consistency, adding few drops milk, if necessary.

NOTE: Use for Butter, White and Pound Cakes.

Browned Butter Frosting

3 tablespoons butter
   (not margarine)
2 cups confectioners' sugar
1 to 2 tablespoons cream or
   milk
¼ teaspoon vanilla

> Frosts tops of 2 layers,
> 12×8-in. cake, 24 cupcakes or
> 3 doz. cookies

Microwave butter in mixing bowl at High 3 to 5 minutes, or until browned, watching closely after 3 minutes. Stir in sugar. Blend in cream and vanilla. Beat until smooth and of spreading consistency, adding a few drops cream, if necessary.

NOTE: Use for Spice, Date, Pumpkin and many other cakes.

Buttercream Frosting

2 tablespoons butter or
   margarine
2 tablespoons cream or milk
⅛ teaspoon salt
2 cups confectioners' sugar
½ teaspoon vanilla or rum
   flavoring

> Frosts tops of 2 layers,
> 12×8-in. cake, 24 cupcakes or
> 3 to 4 doz. cookies

In mixing bowl, combine butter, cream and salt. Microwave at 50% (Medium) 1 to 2 minutes, or until mixture is bubbling. Add sugar and vanilla. Beat until smooth and of spreading consistency, adding few drops cream, if necessary.

Variations:

Coffee Frosting: Add ½ teaspoon, instant coffee to butter mixture before microwaving.

Maple Frosting: Substitute ¼ teaspoon maple flavoring for the vanilla.

NOTE: Use for all cake flavors.

Lemon Frosting

2 tablespoons butter or
    margarine
1 tablespoon cream or milk
1 tablespoon lemon juice
1 teaspoon grated lemon peel
⅛ teaspoon salt
2 cups confectioners' sugar
½ teaspoon vanilla
2 or 3 drops yellow food
    coloring

Frosts tops of 2 layers,
12 × 8-in. cake, 24 cupcakes or,
3 to 4 doz. cookies

In mixing bowl combine butter,
cream, juice, peel and salt.
Microwave at 50% (Medium) 1 to
2 minutes, or until bubbling. Add
sugar, vanilla and coloring. Beat
until smooth and of spreading
consistency, adding few drops
cream; if necessary.

Variation:

Orange Frosting: Substitute 2
tablespoons orange juice for
cream and lemon juice and
orange peel for lemon peel.

NOTE: Use for Ginger, Jam,
Yellow, Banana and
Applesauce Cakes.

Peanut Butter Frosting

2 tablespoons butter or
    margarine
2 tablespoons peanut butter
2 tablespoons cream or milk
⅛ teaspoon salt
2 cups confectioners' sugar
½ teaspoon vanilla

Frosts tops of 2 layers,
12 × 8-in. cake, 24 cupcakes or,
3 to 4 doz. cookies

In mixing bowl combine butter,
peanut butter, cream and salt.
Microwave at 50% (Medium) 1 to
2 minutes, or until mixture is
bubbling. Add sugar and vanilla.
Beat until smooth and of
spreading consistency, adding
few drops cream, if necessary.
Sprinkle frosted cake with finely
chopped peanuts if desired.

NOTE: Use for Chocolate, White
and Peanut Butter Cakes.

Cherry Nut Frosting

2 tablespoons butter or
    margarine
1 tablespoon cream or milk
1 tablespoon cherry juice
⅛ teaspoon salt
2 cups confectioners' sugar
2 tablespoons chopped
    maraschino cherries
2 tablespoons chopped nuts
½ teaspoon vanilla

Frosts tops of 2 layers,
12 × 8-in. cake, 24 cupcakes or,
3 to 4 doz. cookies

In mixing bowl combine butter,
cream, juice and salt.
Microwave at 50% (Medium) 1 to
2 minutes, or until mixture is
boiling. Add sugar, cherries,
nuts and vanilla. Beat until
smooth and of spreading
consistency, adding few drops
cream; if necessary.

NOTE: Use for White, Yellow and
Chocolate Cakes.

Butterscotch Frosting

3 tablespoons butter or
   margarine
3 tablespoons milk
⅓ cup packed brown sugar
⅛ teaspoon salt
2 cups confectioners' sugar
½ teaspoon vanilla

Frosts tops of 2 layers,
12×8-in. cake or
24 cupcakes

In medium mixing bowl,
combine butter, milk, sugar and
salt. Microwave at High 1½ to 4
minutes, or until mixture comes
to a boil, stirring after half the
time. Boil 30 seconds. Add
confectioners' sugar and vanilla.
Beat until smooth and of
spreading consistency, adding
few drops milk, if necessary.

NOTE: Use for Date, Pumpkin,
Banana and Applesauce Cake.

Chocolate Frosting

1 oz. unsweetened chocolate*
   (pre-melted or squares)
2 tablespoons butter or
   margarine
3 tablespoons milk

2 cups confectioners' sugar
½ teaspoon vanilla or
   mint flavoring
⅛ teaspoon salt

Frosts tops of 2 layers,
12×8-in. cake or 24 cupcakes

In small mixing bowl, combine chocolate, butter and milk. Microwave at 50% (Medium) 3 to 4 minutes, or until chocolate is soft and
mixture is thick, stirring after half the time. Stir in remaining ingredients. Let stand 5 to 10 minutes. Beat until smooth and of spreading
consistency, 1 to 3 minutes, adding few drops milk, if necessary.

*If recipe is cut in half use the full amount of chocolate.

Variations:

Choco-Cherry Frosting: Substitute maraschino cherry juice for half
the milk and add 9 maraschino cherries, cut fine, with the sugar.

Chocolate Peanut Frosting: Add 3 tablespoons peanut butter to
chocolate mixture before microwaving. Sprinkle frosted cake with
finely chopped peanuts, if desired.

Chocolate Mallow Frosting: Just before frosting cake, stir in 1½
cups miniature marshmallows. (If frosting a layer cake, remove ¾
cup frosting before adding marshmallows; use to frost the sides.)

Cocoa Frosting: Substitute 3 tablespoons cocoa for chocolate and
increase butter to ¼ cup.

NOTE: Use for Chocolate, White and Yellow Cakes.

How to Make the Right Amount of Frosting

Recipes in this chapter frost the tops of two 9-in. round, 8×8- or 10×6-in. layers, a 12×8-in. cake, 2 to 3 dozen cupcakes or 3 to 4 dozen cookies.

Double the amounts of all the ingredients if you want to frost and fill a two-layer cake, or 3 dozen cupcakes.

Cut ingredients in half to frost tops of 9-in. round, 8×8- or 12×8-in. cake, 1 to 2 dozen cupcakes or 2 to 3 dozen cookies.

Lemon Filling

⅓ cup sugar
1½ tablespoons cornstarch
   Pinch salt
¾ cup water
1 egg yolk, beaten
1 tablespoon butter or
   margarine
2 teaspoons grated lemon
   peel
3 tablespoons lemon juice

     Makes about 1¼ cups

In 4-cup measure or small mixing bowl, combine sugar, cornstarch and salt. Gradually stir in water. Microwave at High 3 to 4 minutes, or until very thick, stirring after 2 minutes, then every minute. Mix a little hot mixture into egg yolk. Blend into remaining sugar mixture. Microwave at 50% (Medium) 1 minute. Stir in butter, peel and lemon juice until smooth. Cover; cool slightly.

Vanilla Cream Filling

¼ cup sugar
2 tablespoons cornstarch
   Pinch salt
1¼ cups milk
2 egg yolks, beaten
1 tablespoon butter or
   margarine
1 teaspoon vanilla

     Makes about 1½ cups

In 4-cup measure or small mixing bowl, combine sugar, cornstarch and salt. Gradually stir in milk. Microwave at High 4 to 7 minutes, or until very thick, stirring after 2 minutes, then every minute. Mix a little hot mixture into egg yolks. Blend into remaining milk mixture. Microwave at 50% (Medium) 1 minute. Stir in butter until smooth. Cover; cool slightly. Stir in vanilla.

Variation:

Chocolate Filling: Increase sugar to ⅓ cup and add 1 oz. unsweetened chocolate to milk mixture before microwaving. If cooked filling is not smooth, beat with rotary beater.

Cookies

Individual Cookies

Many people believe that it is impractical to microwave individual cookies because only 6 to 10 are cooked at a time. In fact, microwaving saves time and energy even though cookies do require constant attention. A full batch of three dozen cookies can be microwaved in about 10 minutes, the time it takes to preheat a conventional oven, and you need only one cookie sheet.

Good cookies require good measuring and mixing techniques. Be sure to read the section Know Your Ingredients & How to Measure Them, page 4.

Most microwaved cookies are soft and chewy. Except for pastry style and bar cookies, it is difficult to make a crisp microwaved cookie. To keep cookies from spreading thin and becom-

ing too tender, the dough must be stiffer than a conventional recipe. If you use a hand mixer, it may be necessary to finish mixing some doughs with a spoon.

Microwaved cookies do not brown. Frosting or dusting them with confectioners' sugar will add eye and appetite appeal. Store frosted cookies flat, or layer with wax paper.

Tips for Microwaving Individual Cookies

Place sheet of wax paper on bottom of microwave baking sheet, large, flat dinner plate or platter, paper plate or pie plate.

Arrange cookies in circle near edge of dish with 1 to 3 in center. Place pastry and rolled cookies close together; space drop and molded cookies at least 2-in. apart. Bake 6 to 9 at a time.

Microwave most cookies at 50% (Medium). A dish of 6 to 10 should be done in 2 to 3 minutes. For less than 6, allow 15 to 30 seconds per cookie.

Increase power to High or 70% (Medium-High) if cookies are still moist and doughy after 2 minutes. Microwave ½ to 1 minute. Bake remaining cookies at the higher power 1½ to 3 minutes.

Do not overbake or cookies will burn in the middle. Surface should be just dry. If 1 or 2 cookies appear unbaked, cut wax paper around cookie and return it to oven.

Slide wax paper with cookies on it to countertop. Re-use baking dish for remaining cookies. When cookies are cool, remove from wax paper and store in air-tight container.

Chocolate Chip Cookies

½ cup butter or margarine
⅔ cup packed brown sugar
 1 egg
 1 teaspoon soda
 1 teaspoon vanilla
½ teaspoon salt
 2 cups all-purpose flour
½ to 1 cup chocolate chips
½ cup chopped nuts, optional

Makes about 3 dozen

Mix butter, sugar, egg, soda, vanilla and salt until light and fluffy. Stir in remaining ingredients. Drop 5 to 8 rounded measuring teaspoonfuls in large ring on wax paper on microwave-proof baking sheet, large dinner plate, pie plate or paper plate. Drop 1 or 2 in center.

Microwave at 50% (Medium) 1 to 4 minutes, or just until dry on surface, rotating ¼ turn after 1 minute, then every 30 seconds. (If necessary, rotate after first 30 seconds.) Remove cookies as they appear done. Remove wax paper with cookies on it to countertop; cool.

Old-Time Raisin Drops

¾ cup apricot or orange juice
  or water
 1 cup raisins
 1 cup quick-cooking
  rolled oats
½ cup shortening
¾ cup sugar
¼ cup molasses
 2 eggs

1 tablespoon grated orange
  peel
1 teaspoon baking powder
1 teaspoon soda
1 teaspoon salt
1 teaspoon cinnamon
1 teaspoon vanilla
¼ teaspoon cloves
2½ cups all-purpose flour

Makes 4 to 5 dozen

In mixing bowl, combine juice and raisins. Microwave at High 2 to 5 minutes, or until mixture comes to full boil. Cool 10 minutes. Mix in remaining ingredients except flour. Blend in flour. Drop 5 to 8 rounded measuring teaspoonfuls in large ring on wax paper on microwave-proof baking sheet, large dinner plate, pie plate or paper plate. Drop 1 or 2 in center.

Microwave at 50% (Medium) 1½ to 4½ minutes, or just until dry on surface, rotating ¼ turn every 45 seconds. Remove cookies as they appear done. Remove wax paper with cookies on it to countertop; cool.

| Basic Cookies | Chip Cookies | Coconut Drops |

Six-Way Butter Cookies

½ cup butter or margarine
½ cup sugar
 1 egg
 2 tablespoons milk or cream
 2 teaspoons baking powder
 1 or 2 teaspoons vanilla
½ teaspoon salt
 2 cups all-purpose flour

Makes 2½ to 3 dozen

Variations:

Chip Cookies: Stir ½ to 1 cup chocolate chips and ½ cup chopped nuts, optional, into dough.

Coconut Drops: Stir 1 cup plain, toasted or colored flaked coconut and ½ teaspoon almond extract into dough.

Orange-Raisin Cookies: Stir ½ to 1 cup raisins and 2 teaspoons grated orange peel into dough.

Nut Drops: Stir 1 cup chopped nuts into dough.

Spice Drops: Add 2 tablespoons molasses, 1 teaspoon cinnamon and ¼ teaspoon each nutmeg, ginger and cloves.

How to Microwave Six-Way Butter Cookies

Place all ingredients except flour in mixing bowl; blend well. Add flour. Beat at low speed until dough forms. Drop 6 to 8 rounded measuring teaspoonfuls in large ring on wax paper on baking sheet, dinner plate, pie plate or paper plate. Drop 1 in center.

Make thinner cookies, if desired, by flattening unbaked cookies to about ¼ in. with lightly greased bottom of glass dipped in plain, cinnamon or colored sugar.

Microwave at 50% (Medium) 1½ to 3½ minutes, or just until dry on surface, rotating ¼ turn every 30 seconds to 1 minute. Remove cookies as they appear done. Remove wax paper with cookies on it to countertop; cool. Frost with a complementary frosting or roll in confectioners' sugar.

Orange-Raisin Cookies   Nut Drops   Spice Drops

Salted Peanut Cookies

½ cup shortening
 1 cup packed brown sugar
 2 eggs
 1 teaspoon vanilla
½ teaspoon soda
½ teaspoon baking powder
½ teaspoon salt
 2 cups all-purpose flour
 2 cups quick-cooking
    rolled oats
 1 cup rice crispy cereal
 1 cup salted Spanish peanuts

Makes about 5 dozen

Mix shortening, sugar, eggs,
vanilla, soda, baking powder
and salt until light and fluffy.
Blend in flour. Stir in remaining
ingredients. Drop 5 to 8 rounded
measuring teaspoonfuls in large
ring on wax paper on microwave-
proof baking sheet, large dinner
plate, pie plate or paper plate.
Drop 1 or 2 in center.

Microwave at 50% (Medium) 1 to
3½ minutes, or just until dry on
surface, rotating ¼ turn every 30
seconds. Remove cookies as
they appear done. Remove wax
paper with cookies on it to
countertop or wire rack; cool.

77

Swedish Butter Cookies

2 cups all-purpose flour
½ cup confectioners' sugar
½ teaspoon cream of tartar
½ teaspoon soda
¼ teaspoon salt
½ teaspoon almond extract
½ teaspoon vanilla
½ cup butter or margarine, room temperature
1 egg
40 to 45 whole unblanched almonds

Makes about 4 dozen

Variations:

Swedish Vienna Pole Cookies: Omit almonds. Make deep indentation down center of each strip with knife handle. Microwave as directed below. Immediately spoon scant 2 tablespoons jelly down center of each strip. Dust with confectioners' sugar while warm, or frost with a thin Vanilla Icing, page 92. When cool, cut into 1-in. strips.

Swedish Butter Balls: Shape dough into 1-in. balls. Place 6 to 8 in large ring on wax paper on baking dish, dinner plate, pie plate or paper plate. Place 1 or 2 in center. Press almond firmly into top of each ball. Microwave at 50% (Medium) 1 to 3½ minutes; rotate ¼ turn every 30 seconds.

How to Microwave Swedish Butter Cookies

Place all ingredients except almonds in mixing bowl. Beat at low speed until dough forms. Divide dough into 5 equal parts.

Shape 1 part into 9-in. strip on 4-in. wide strip of wax paper. Place strip, with wax paper underneath, on baking sheet or in 12×8-in. baking dish.

Press 8 or 9 almonds firmly into strip of dough about ⅛-in. apart down center.

Peanut Butter Cookies

½ cup shortening
1 cup peanut butter
1 cup packed brown sugar
2 eggs
½ teaspoon soda
½ teaspoon salt
½ teaspoon vanilla
2¼ cups all-purpose flour

Makes 4 to 5 dozen

Mix all ingredients except flour until light and fluffy. Blend in flour. Shape dough into 1-in. balls. Place 6 to 8 balls in large ring on wax paper on microwave-proof baking sheet, large dinner plate, pie plate or paper plate. Place 1 or 2 in center. Flatten to about ½-in. with fork. Microwave at 50% (Medium) 1 to 4½ minutes, rotating ¼ turn after 1 minute, then every 30 seconds. Remove wax paper with cookies on it to countertop or wire rack. Top each with ½ teaspoon each jelly and peanut butter, if desired.

Variations:

Peanut Butter Poles: Divide dough into 9 equal parts. Shape 1 part into 9-in. strip on 4-in. wide strip of wax paper. (See photo directions for Swedish Butter Cookies.) Place strip, with wax paper underneath, on microwave-proof baking sheet or in 12×8-in. baking dish. Flatten to about ½-in. with fork.

Microwave at 50% (Medium) 1½ to 3 minutes, or just until dry on surface, rotating ¼ turn every minute. Carefully remove wax paper with cookie strip on it to countertop. When almost cool, cut diagonally into 1-in. strips. Cool completely. Repeat with remaining dough.

Chocolate Chip Peanut Butter Cookies: Add ½ to 1 cup chocolate chips with flour.

Peanutty Peanut Butter Cookies: Add ½ cup chopped salted peanuts with flour.

Microwave at 50% (Medium) 1½ to 3½ minutes, or just until dry on surface, rotating ½ turn every minute. Carefully remove wax paper with cookie strip on it to countertop or wire rack.

Sprinkle with confectioners' sugar while warm. When almost cool, cut diagonally between almonds into 1-in. strips. Repeat with remaining dough.

Chocolate Crackles

¼ cup butter or margarine
2 ounces unsweetened chocolate, pre-melted or solid
1 cup granulated sugar
2 eggs
2 teaspoons baking powder
1 teaspoon vanilla
½ teaspoon salt
2 cups all-purpose flour
½ cup chopped nuts, optional
Confectioners' sugar

Makes about 4 dozen

In mixing bowl, combine butter and chocolate. Microwave at 50% (Medium) 1 to 4 minutes, or until melted; blend well. Beat in granulated sugar, eggs, baking powder, vanilla and salt. Stir in flour and nuts. Refrigerate overnight or at least 8 hours.

Shape dough into 1-in. balls. Roll in confectioners' sugar. Place 6 to 8 balls in large ring on wax paper on baking sheet, dinner plate, pie plate or paper plate. Place 1 in center. Microwave at 50% (Medium) 1¼ to 3 minutes, or just until surface is dry, rotating ¼ turn every 30 seconds. Remove wax paper with cookies on it to countertop; cool.

Pfeffernuesse Balls

½ cup sugar
½ cup shortening
½ cup light molasses
¼ cup water
½ teaspoon instant coffee, optional
3 eggs
1 teaspoon soda
1 teaspoon cinnamon
½ teaspoon salt
½ teaspoon ginger
¼ teaspoon cloves
4 cups all-purpose flour

Makes about 5 dozen

In mixing bowl, combine sugar, shortening, molasses, water and coffee. Microwave at High 5 minutes, stirring after 2 minutes. Cool 10 minutes. Add remaining ingredients; blend well. Refrigerate overnight or at least 4 hours.

Shape dough into 1-in. balls. Place 5 to 8 balls in large ring on wax paper on baking sheet, dinner plate, pie plate or paper plate. Microwave at 50% (Medium) 1 to 4 minutes, or just until surface is dry; rotate ¼ turn every 30 seconds. Remove wax paper with cookies on it to countertop; cool. Serve as is or roll in confectioners' sugar or frost with Orange Frosting, page 69.

Shape refrigerated cookie dough into 1-in. balls with palms of hands. Roll in confectioners' sugar as recipe directs.

Scotchy Oat Slices

½ cup butter, margarine or
    shortening
1 cup packed brown sugar
2 eggs
1 teaspoon soda
1 teaspoon salt
1 teaspoon cinnamon, optional
1 teaspoon vanilla
2 cups all-purpose flour
3 cups quick-cooking
    rolled oats

Makes 6 to 7 dozen

Place all ingredients except flour
and oats in large mixing bowl;
blend well. Stir in flour, then oats.
Divide dough in half. Shape each
into 10-in. rectangular roll. Wrap in
wax paper. Refrigerate overnight.

Cut rolls into about ¼-in. slices.
Place 6 to 8 slices in large ring
on wax paper on baking sheet,
dinner plate, pie plate or paper
plate. Place 1 in center.
Microwave at 50% (Medium) 1 to
2¾ minutes, or just until dry on
surface, rotating ¼ turn every
minute. Remove wax paper with
cookies on it to countertop; cool.

Pepperkakor Slices

1 cup shortening
¾ cup sugar
1 egg
½ cup light molasses
1 teaspoon soda
1 teaspoon cinnamon
1 teaspoon ginger
½ teaspoon cloves
2 teaspoons grated orange
    peel, optional
4 cups all-purpose flour
1 cup (2½ oz.) almond slices

Makes 8 to 9 dozen

Place all ingredients except flour
and almonds in large mixing
bowl; blend well. Add flour and
almonds. Beat at low speed until
dough forms. Divide dough into 4
equal parts. Shape each part into
6-in. rectangular roll. Wrap in wax
paper. Refrigerate overnight.

Cut rolls into about ⅛-in. slices.
Place 7 to 10 slices in large ring
on wax paper on baking sheet,
dinner plate, pie plate, or paper
plate. Place 1 or 2 in center.

Microwave at 50% (Medium) 1¼
to 3½ minutes, or just until dry on
surface, rotating ¼ turn after 1
minute, then every 30 seconds.
Remove wax paper with cookies
on it to countertop; cool.

Shape dough into rectangular
roll on wax paper, smoothing
sides with straight edge. Roll up in
wax paper and refrigerate overnight. To slice dough, use a very
sharp knife and a sawing motion.

Wheat Sweets

½ cup butter or margarine,
  room temperature
2 tablespoons shortening
1½ cups whole wheat flour
¼ cup sugar
1 teaspoon anise seed or
  fennel and/or grated
  orange peel
½ teaspoon salt
¼ cup cold water

Makes 50

In mixing bowl, combine all ingredients except water. Beat at low speed or cut with pastry blender until particles resemble coarse crumbs. Gradually stir in water while stirring with fork just until dough forms. Chill, if necessary, for easier handling.

Roll out dough, half at a time, on floured surface to 10-in. square. Sprinkle lightly with sugar, if desired. Cut into 2-in. squares. Place 5 to 9 squares close together in ring on wax paper on microwave-proof baking sheet, large dinner plate, pie plate or paper plate. Place 1 to 3 in center.

Microwave at High 1½ to 4 minutes, or until dry and slightly firm to touch, rotating ¼ turn after 1 and 2 minutes, then every 30 seconds.* Remove to wire rack.

*If microwaving less than 6 cookies, allow 20 to 50 seconds per cookie.

French Pastry Cookies

2 cups all-purpose flour
½ teaspoon salt
¼ teaspoon cream of tartar
½ cup butter or margarine, room
  temperature
¼ cup shortening
⅓ cup half & half
1 teaspoon vanilla
3 tablespoons sugar*
½ teaspoon cinnamon

Makes about 3 dozen

In mixing bowl, combine flour, salt, cream of tartar, butter and shortening. Beat at low speed or cut with pastry blender until particles are fine. Combine half & half and vanilla. Gradually stir into flour mixture with fork just until dough forms. (Add more cream if needed.)

Roll out dough on floured surface to ⅛-in. thickness. Cut into 2½- to 3-in. rounds. Combine sugar and cinnamon; sprinkle generously over rounds. Place 6 to 10 rounds close together in large ring on wax paper on microwave-proof baking sheet, large dinner plate, pie plate or paper plate. Place 1 or 2 in center.

Microwave at High 1½ to 5 minutes, or until dry and opaque, rotating ¼ turn every 30 seconds or as needed. Remove cookies to wire rack as they appear done.

*During the holiday season, substitute red and green sugars for cinnamon-sugar.

Caramel Candy Toppers

¾ cup butter or margarine, room
    temperature
2 cups all-purpose flour
½ cup sugar
¼ teaspoon salt
3 tablespoons milk
3 drops yellow food coloring
1 teaspoon vanilla

Topping:
½ lb. light colored caramels
    (about 28)
1 tablespoon milk
¼ cup butter or margarine
1 cup confectioners' sugar
¾ cup chopped nuts

Frosting:
½ cup chocolate chips
1 tablespoon shortening

Makes 50

How to Microwave Caramel Candy Toppers

Place butter, flour, sugar and salt in mixing bowl. Beat at low speed or cut with pastry blender until particles are fine. Combine milk, food coloring and vanilla.

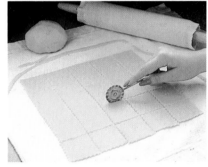

Gradually stir into flour mixture with fork just until dough forms. Roll out dough, half at a time, on floured surface to 10-in. square. Cut into 2-in. squares.

Place 6 to 10 squares close together in large ring on wax paper on baking sheet, large dinner plate, pie plate or paper plate. Place 1 to 3 in center.

Microwave at High 1½ to 4½ minutes, or until cookies are slightly puffy and dry; rotate ¼ turn after 1 and 2 minutes, then every 30 seconds. Remove cookies as they appear done.

Topping: Place caramels, milk and butter in small bowl. Microwave at High 2 to 4 minutes, stirring every minute. Stir in sugar and nuts. Place a teaspoonful of topping on each square.

Frosting: Place chips and shortening in small bowl. Microwave at 50% (Medium) 2 to 4 minutes, or until chips are soft and shiny; mix well. Frost top of each cookie.

Bar Cookies

Bar cookies are a microwaving specialty. Many of these recipes can be microwaved in 5 to 8 minutes, less time than it takes to preheat a conventional oven. The recipes include traditional favorites, popular cookies in a bar shape, and candy-like bars for special occasions.

Cut bars in generous pieces for a lunch box. For gift giving, or an assorted cookie tray, cut smaller pieces and be sure to include some rich, candy flavored bars.

For easy storage, slip the dish of bars into a plastic bag.

Tips for Microwaving Bars

No dish preparation is needed, unless called for in recipe. Shield corners with foil during first half of microwaving if they tend to overbake in your oven.

Set dish on inverted saucer during microwaving, and rotate ¼ turn frequently to help bars bake evenly and quickly.

Touch top in center and several other places. It should spring back. A small amount of moisture on surface will dry.

Check for doneness on center bottom. Very little unbaked batter should appear. Layered bars should appear cooked.

Let stand directly on countertop 5 to 10 minutes to complete cooking. Frost bars warm. Heat improves the flavor of frosting.

Cut with sharp knife when completely cool. For crisp bars, quarter and remove each quarter to firm surface with pancake turner to complete cutting.

Fudgy Brownies

2 ounces unsweetened
  chocolate, pre-melted or
  solid
½ cup butter or margarine
1 cup packed brown or
  granulated sugar
¾ cup all-purpose flour

2 eggs
½ teaspoon baking powder
½ teaspoon vanilla
¼ teaspoon salt
½ cup finely chopped nuts,
  optional

Makes 8×8- or 10×6-in. dish

In mixing bowl, combine chocolate, butter and sugar. Microwave at 50% (Medium) 2 to 4 minutes, or until melted. Blend well. Add remaining ingredients; beat until well blended. Spread in 8×8- or 10×6-in. baking dish.

Place dish on inverted saucer in microwave oven. Microwave at High 4 to 7 minutes, or until done, rotating ¼ turn after 2, 4 and 5 minutes. Cool directly on countertop and frost with Chocolate Frosting, page 70.

Variations:

Rocky Road Brownies: Sprinkle hot bars with 1 cup miniature marshmallows. Frost with Chocolate Frosting, page 70. (Frosting should be thin enough to drizzle.)

Cherry Brownies: Add ¼ cup cut-up maraschino cherries to batter. Add 6 finely cut cherries to frosting and substitute cherry juice for milk.

Peanut Brownies: Decrease butter to ¼ cup, plus 2 tablespoons and add ¼ cup peanut butter to batter. Use peanuts for nuts. Add 1 tablespoon peanut butter to frosting. Sprinkle frosted brownies with ¼ cup chopped peanuts.

Macaroon Brownies: Combine 2 cups flaked coconut, ¼ cup sugar and 2 tablespoons water. Prepare batter. Spread ⅔ in baking dish. Top with coconut mixture. Spoon remaining batter onto top, allowing coconut to show through.

Blonde Brownies

½ cup butter or margarine
¾ cup packed brown sugar
2 eggs
¾ cup all-purpose flour
½ teaspoon baking powder
½ teaspoon vanilla
¼ teaspoon salt
¼ cup chopped nuts
½ cup chocolate chips, divided

Makes 8×8- or 10×6-in. dish

Microwave butter in mixing bowl at High 45 to 60 seconds, or until melted. Stir in sugar thoroughly. Stir in remaining ingredients except chips. Spread in 8×8- or 10×6-in. baking dish. Sprinkle with ¼ cup chips. Shield corners of dish with triangles of foil.

Place dish on inverted saucer in microwave oven. Microwave at High 4 minutes, rotating ¼ turn every 2 minutes. Sprinkle with ¼ cup chips. Microwave at High 1 to 3 minutes, rotating ¼ turn every minute. Cool directly on countertop 30 minutes. When cool, sprinkle with confectioners' sugar or frost with Browned Butter Frosting, page 68.

Date-filled Bars

Date Filling:
 1 cup dates, halved
 ⅓ cup water
 3 tablespoons sugar
 1 tablespoon lemon juice

Cookie Base:
 ½ cup butter or margarine
 ⅔ cup packed brown sugar
 ¼ teaspoon salt
 1 cup quick-cooking rolled oats
 1 cup all-purpose flour

Makes 8×8-in. dish

Variation:

Mincemeat Bars: Substitute 1 cup prepared mincemeat for date mixture.

How to Microwave Date-filled Bars

Combine filling ingredients in mixing bowl. Microwave at High 3 to 5 minutes, or until thick and smooth, stirring every minute.

Mix butter, sugar and salt. Add oats and flour. Beat at low speed until particles are fine. Reserve 1 cup. Press remaining crumbly mixture in 8×8-in. baking dish.

Place dish on inverted saucer in microwave oven. Microwave at 50% (Medium) 3 to 7 minutes, or just until done, rotating ¼ turn every 2 minutes.

Decrease power to 30% (Low) if base starts to boil hard in spots after 1 to 1½ minutes.

Spoon date mixture over base; spread carefully. Sprinkle with reserved crumbly mixture.

Microwave at High 4 to 8 minutes, or until crumbly mixture is cooked; rotating ½ turn every 2 minutes. (Top with whipped cream and serve as a dessert.)

Caramel Nut Bars

¾ cup butter or margarine,
   divided
⅔ cup packed brown sugar
¼ teaspoon salt
1 cup quick-cooking rolled oats
1 cup all-purpose flour
½ lb. caramel candies
   (about 28)
2 tablespoons milk
1 cup confectioners' sugar
¼ cup chopped nuts

Makes 8×8-in. dish

Mix ½ cup butter, brown sugar and salt. Add oats and flour. Beat at low speed until particles are fine. Reserve 1 cup. Press remaining crumbly mixture in 8×8-in. dish. Place dish on inverted saucer in microwave oven. Microwave at 50% (Medium) 3 to 7 minutes, or just until done; rotate ¼ turn every 2 minutes.

In 4-cup measure or small mixing bowl, combine caramels, milk and ¼ cup butter. Microwave at 50% (Medium) 2 to 5½ minutes, or until caramels are soft, stirring every 2 minutes. Blend well. Stir in confectioners' sugar and nuts. Spread over base. Sprinkle with reserved crumbly mixture. Microwave 3 to 8 minutes, or until topping bubbles in several places, rotating ¼ turn every 3 minutes. Cool directly on countertop.

Lemon Cheesecake Bars

½ cup butter or margarine
½ cup packed brown sugar
¼ teaspoon salt
1 cup quick-cooking rolled oats
1 cup all-purpose flour
1 package (8 oz.) cream
   cheese
⅓ cup granulated sugar
1 egg
1 tablespoon grated lemon peel
1 tablespoon lemon juice
2 tablespoons milk

Makes 8×8-in. dish

Mix butter, brown sugar and salt. Add oats and flour. Beat at low speed until particles are fine. Reserve 1 cup. Press remaining crumbly mixture in 8×8-in. baking dish. Microwave at 50% (Medium) 3 to 7½ minutes, or just until almost done, rotating ¼ turn every 2 minutes.

Microwave cream cheese in small mixing bowl at 50% (Medium) 30 seconds. Add remaining ingredients; blend well. Spread over base. Sprinkle with reserved crumbly mixture. Microwave at High 6 to 10 minutes, or until firm in center, rotating ¼ turn every 3 minutes. Cool and refrigerate.

Chocolate-filled Bars

¾ cup butter or margarine
1 cup packed brown sugar
½ teaspoon salt
2 cups quick-cooking rolled
   oats
1½ cups all-purpose flour
1 can (14 oz.) sweetened
   condensed milk
1 cup semisweet chocolate
   chips
½ cup chopped nuts, optional

Makes 12×8-in. dish

Mix butter, sugar and salt. Add oats and flour. Beat at low speed until particles are fine. Reserve 1½ cups. Press remaining crumbly mixture in 12×8-in. baking dish. Place dish on inverted saucer in microwave oven. Microwave at 50% (Medium) 6 to 10 minutes, or just until almost done; rotate ¼ turn every 2 or 3 minutes.

Microwave milk in 4-cup measure or small mixing bowl at High 1 minute. Stir in chips and nuts. (If chips do not melt, microwave 30 seconds.) Spread chocolate mixture over base. Sprinkle with reserved crumbly mixture. Microwave at High 6 to 9 minutes, or until chocolate mixture bubbles in several places, rotating ¼ turn every 3 minutes. Cool directly on countertop.

Dream Bars

¼ cup, plus 2 tablespoons
    butter or margarine
1¼ cups packed brown sugar,
    divided
  1 cup all-purpose flour

2 eggs
1 teaspoon vanilla
½ teaspoon baking powder
1½ cups flaked coconut,
    divided

Makes 8×8-in. dish

How to Microwave Dream Bars

Mix butter and ¼ cup sugar, in small mixing bowl. Beat in flour at low speed until crumbly. Press in 8×8-in. baking dish.

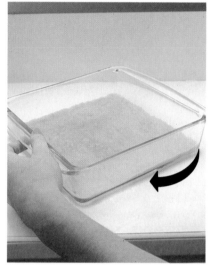

Microwave at 50% (Medium) 3 to 7 minutes, or until almost done, rotating ¼ turn every 2 minutes.

Combine 1 cup sugar, eggs, vanilla, baking powder and 1 cup coconut. Beat at medium speed until well blended. Spread over base.

Microwave at 50% (Medium) 5 to 10 minutes, or until almost done in center; rotate ¼ turn every 2 minutes. Sprinkle with ½ cup coconut. Microwave 1 to 3 minutes, or until set. Cool directly on countertop.

88

Chinese Chews

2 eggs	⅔ cup all-purpose flour
⅔ cup sugar	1 cup finely cut dates
1 teaspoon vanilla	1 cup chopped nuts
½ teaspoon baking powder	Confectioners' sugar
½ teaspoon salt	

Makes 8×8-in. dish

How to Microwave Chinese Chews

Beat eggs, sugar, vanilla, baking powder and salt until thick and ivory colored. Combine flour, dates and nuts. Stir into egg mixture. Spread in 8×8-in. dish. Shield corners with foil.

Place dish on inverted saucer in microwave oven. Microwave at High 5 to 8 minutes, or until almost dry on top, rotating ¼ turn after 2 minutes, then every minute. Remove foil after 4 minutes.

Cool bars directly on countertop. Cut into about 1-in. squares. Roll squares in hands to shape into balls.

Place balls in plastic bag; add about ¼ cup confectioners' sugar. Turn bag over and around until balls are coated.

Orange Pecan Bars

¾ cup all-purpose flour
¼ cup butter or margarine,
    room temperature
¼ cup packed brown sugar
¼ cup granulated sugar
 2 eggs
⅓ cup dairy sour cream
½ teaspoon baking powder
¼ teaspoon soda
¼ teaspoon salt
 1 tablespoon grated orange
    peel
¼ cup chopped pecans or nuts

Makes 8×8- or 10×6-in. dish

Place all ingredients in mixing
bowl. Beat at low speed 1
minute. Spread in 8×8- or 10×6-
in. baking dish.

Place dish on inverted saucer in
microwave oven. Microwave at
High 3½ to 7 minutes, or until
done, rotating ¼ turn after 2, 4
and 5 minutes. Frost while warm
with Orange Frosting, page 69.

Sour Cream Chocolate Bars

⅔ cup all-purpose flour
½ cup sugar
½ cup butter or margarine,
    room temperature
¼ cup cocoa
½ cup dairy sour cream
 2 eggs
½ teaspoon soda
½ teaspoon vanilla
¼ teaspoon salt

Makes 12×8-in. dish

Place all ingredients in mixing
bowl. Blend at low speed, then
beat at medium speed 2
minutes. Spread in 12×8-in.
baking dish.*

Place dish on inverted saucer in
microwave oven. Microwave at
High 5 to 8 minutes, or until
done, rotating ¼ turn after 2, 4
and 5 minutes. Cool directly on
countertop. Frost with Chocolate
Frosting, page 70.

*May also be microwaved in two
8×8- or 10×6-in. baking dishes.
Microwave 1 dish at a time 2 to 5
minutes, rotating ¼ turn every
1½ minutes.

Ginger Cream Bars

¾ cup all-purpose flour
⅓ cup sugar
½ teaspoon soda
½ teaspoon ginger
¼ teaspoon salt
¼ teaspoon nutmeg
¼ teaspoon cinnamon
⅛ teaspoon cloves
¼ cup shortening
¼ cup light molasses
2 tablespoons hot water
2 eggs

Makes 12×8-in. dish

Place all ingredients in mixing bowl. Blend at low speed 1 minute. Spread in 12×8-in. baking dish.*

Place dish on inverted saucer in microwave oven. Microwave at High 4 to 7 minutes, or until done, rotating ¼ turn every 2 minutes. Frost while warm with Orange Frosting, page 69.

*May also be microwaved in two 8×8- or 10×6-in. baking dishes. Microwave 1 dish at a time 5 to 7 minutes, rotating ¼ turn every 1½ minutes.

Date-Nut Creams

1 cup all-purpose flour
¼ cup butter or margarine, room temperature
½ cup packed brown sugar
2 eggs
½ cup dairy sour cream
½ teaspoon vanilla
½ teaspoon soda
¼ teaspoon salt
½ cup finely cut dates
¼ cup chopped nuts

Makes 12×8-in. dish

Place all ingredients in mixing bowl. Blend at low speed 1 minute. Spread in 12×8-in. baking dish.*

Place dish on inverted saucer in microwave oven. Microwave at High 5 to 8 minutes, or until done, rotating ¼ turn every 2 minutes. Frost while warm with Browned Butter Frosting, page 68.

*May also be microwaved in two 8×8- or 10×6-in. baking dishes. Microwave 1 dish at a time, 3 to 5 minutes, rotating ¼ turn every 1½ minutes.

Southern Lane Bars

15 graham cracker squares
 3 eggs
 1 cup packed brown sugar
½ cup milk
½ cup butter or margarine,
   melted
 1 cup flaked coconut
 1 cup chopped nuts
 1 cup graham cracker crumbs
 1 teaspoon vanilla

Makes 13×9-in. dish

Vanilla Icing:*
 2 tablespoons butter or
   margarine
 2 cups confectioners' sugar
 2 to 3 tablespoons milk or strong
   coffee
½ teaspoon vanilla

*Icing may be used to ice or glaze coffeecakes and tube cakes. Prepare half the recipe.

How to Microwave Southern Lane Bars

Line bottom of 13×9-in. baking dish with graham cracker squares, cutting as necessary to fit. In 2-qt. mixing bowl or casserole, combine eggs, sugar, milk and butter; beat well.

Microwave at High 2 to 5 minutes, or until mixture is very hot and starts to thicken on sides, stirring every 2 minutes.

Decrease power to 50% (Medium). Microwave 3 to 6 minutes, or until very thick, stirring every minute. Mixture will not be smooth.

◄Choco-Scotch Fingers

½ cup butter or margarine
⅔ cup packed brown sugar
2 cups quick-cooking rolled
    oats
½ cup chopped nuts or flaked
    coconut
1 teaspoon vanilla

Topping:
½ cup chocolate chips
¼ cup peanut butter

Makes 8×8-in. dish

Microwave butter in 1½- or 2-qt. mixing bowl or casserole at High 45 to 60 seconds, or until melted. Blend in sugar. Stir in remaining ingredients. Spread in greased 8×8-in. baking dish.

Place dish on inverted saucer in microwave oven. Microwave at High 3 to 6 minutes, or until bubbly all over, rotating ¼ turn after 2 minutes, then every minute. Cool 2 minutes; sprinkle with chips and drop small spoonfuls of peanut butter here and there. When soft, spread to frost, leaving marbled effect. Cut into strips with sharp knife when frosting is partially firm.

Stir in remaining ingredients except Icing. Spoon over crackers; spread carefully. Cool slightly before frosting.

Microwave butter in small mixing bowl at High 30 to 45 seconds, or until melted. Stir in sugar. Blend in milk gradually until of spreading consistency. Stir in vanilla. Frost bars.

Cereal Peanut Crunch

1 pound candy coating, any
    flavor
½ cup peanut butter
2 cups ready-to-eat cereal
    (do not use bran or
    sugar-coated cereals)
1 cup salted peanuts

Makes 1½ pounds (36 pieces)

If candy coating is in solid piece, break into squares. Place squares and peanut butter in single layer in 2-qt. casserole. Microwave at 50% (Medium) 3 to 5 minutes, or until squares are soft, stirring after 3 minutes. Stir until completely melted. Stir in cereal and peanuts. Spread in 9-in. square on wax paper. When firm, cut into 1½-in. squares with sharp knife.

Caramel O Bars

14 or 16 oz. caramel candies
¼ cup water
½ cup peanut butter

4 cups ready-to-eat oat cereal
  circles
1 cup salted peanuts

Topping:
 1 cup chocolate chips
¼ cup peanut butter
2 tablespoons shortening

Makes 13×9- or 12×8-in. dish

How to Microwave Caramel O Bars

Combine caramels, water and peanut butter in large mixing bowl. Microwave at High 3 to 5 minutes, or until melted and smooth, stirring after 2 minutes, then every minute.

Stir in cereal and peanuts. Press mixture in well-buttered 13×9- or 12×8-in. baking dish.

Place topping ingredients in 2-cup measure or small bowl. Microwave at 50% (Medium) 2 to 4 minutes, or until chips are soft; blend well. Spread over bars.

Peanut Butter-ups

1 cup butter or margarine
1 cup peanut butter
2 cups graham cracker crumbs
½ cup finely chopped peanuts,
    optional
2 to 2½ cups confectioners'
    sugar
1 cup chocolate chips
2 tablespoons shortening

Makes 12×8- or 13×9-in. dish

In 2-qt. mixing bowl or casserole, combine butter and peanut butter. Microwave at High 1½ to 2½ minutes or until melted. Blend well. Mix in crumbs, peanuts and sugar until mixture is very stiff. Press firmly in buttered 12×8- or 13×9-in. dish.

In small bowl, combine chips and shortening. Microwave at 50% (Medium) 2½ to 4 minutes, or until chips are shiny and soft. Blend well. Drizzle over bars, spreading carefully. Cool completely before cutting.

Cereal Mallow Bars

¼ cup plus 2 tablespoons
    butter or margarine
1 package (10 oz.) miniature
    marshmallows
¼ cup peanut butter

6 cups cereal checks
2 cups salted peanuts

Topping:
1 cup chocolate chips
¼ cup peanut butter

Makes 13×9-in. dish

Microwave butter in 3-qt. mixing bowl or casserole at High 45 to 60 seconds, or until melted. Stir in marshmallows and peanut butter. Microwave at High 1½ to 2 minutes, or until melted, stirring after 1 minute. Stir until smooth. Add cereal and peanuts; stir with meat fork or wooden spoon until well coated. Press mixture in buttered 13×9- or 12×8-in. baking dish with back of large spoon. (Dip spoon in cold water or coat lightly with butter to prevent sticking.)

Place topping ingredients in small bowl. Microwave at 50% (Medium) 2½ to 4 minutes, or until chips are shiny and soft; blend well. Drizzle over bars, spreading carefully. Cool before cutting.

Graham Toffees

1 tablespoon butter or
   margarine
9 graham cracker squares
½ cup butter or margarine
½ cup packed brown sugar
½ cup almond slices or other
   chopped nuts
½ cup milk chocolate or
   semisweet chocolate chips

Makes 8×8-in. dish

How to Microwave Graham Toffees

Microwave 1 tablespoon butter in 8×8-in. baking dish at High ½ to 1¼ minutes. Spread over bottom and ¼ in. up sides.

Line bottom of dish with graham cracker squares, cutting as necessary to fit.

Combine ½ cup butter and sugar in 4-cup measure or small bowl. Microwave at High 1 minute. Beat with wire whip until smooth. Microwave 2 minutes.

Pour over crackers; spread carefully. Sprinkle with almonds. Microwave at High 1½ to 3 minutes, or until mixture boils 1 minute; rotate ¼ turn every 30 seconds.

Cool 2 minutes then sprinkle with chocolate. When soft, spread to frost bars.

Loosen edges and cut into quarters, then remove each quarter to cutting surface; cut into small pieces. For crisp toffee store in refrigerator.

Peanutty Butterscotch Toppers

9 graham cracker squares
½ cup sugar
1 cup light corn syrup
1 cup butterscotch or chocolate chips
1 cup peanut butter
1 cup salted peanuts or other salted nuts

Makes 8×8- or 9×9-in. dish

Line bottom of 8- or 9-in. square baking dish with graham cracker squares, cutting as necessary to fit. In 1½- to 2-qt. mixing bowl or casserole, combine sugar and syrup. Microwave at High 4 to 6 minutes, or until mixture boils 3 minutes, stirring every 2 minutes. Stir in remaining ingredients. Pour over crackers; spread carefully. Refrigerate until firm.

Date Confections

½ cup butter or margarine
1 cup sugar
⅓ cup all-purpose flour
½ teaspoon salt
2 eggs
1 cup dates, halved
3 cups rice crispy cereal
1 cup chopped nuts
1 teaspoon vanilla
  Confectioners' sugar

Makes 9×9-in. dish

Microwave butter in 2-qt. mixing bowl or casserole 45 to 60 seconds, or until melted. Blend in sugar, flour, salt and eggs thoroughly. Stir in dates. Microwave at High 3½ to 6 minutes, or until very thick, stirring every 2 minutes. Cool 5 minutes.

In large mixing bowl, combine cereal and nuts. Stir in date mixture and vanilla until all ingredients are well distributed. Spread in 9×9-in. baking dish. Refrigerate until chilled. To serve, cut in 1-in. squares and coat with confectioners' sugar.

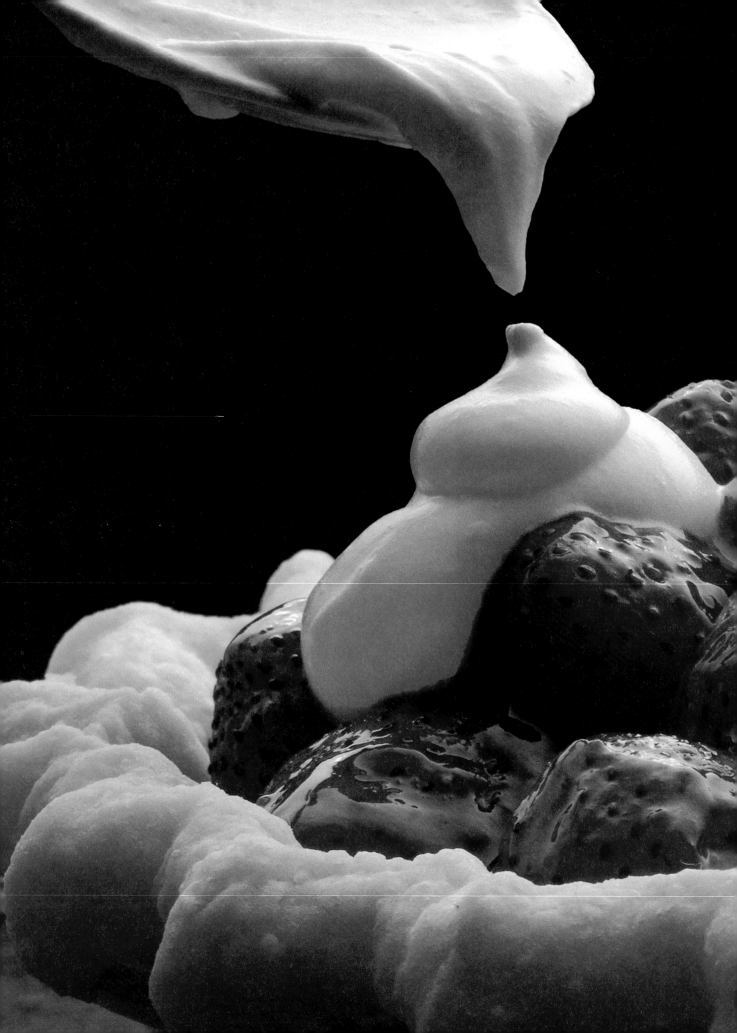

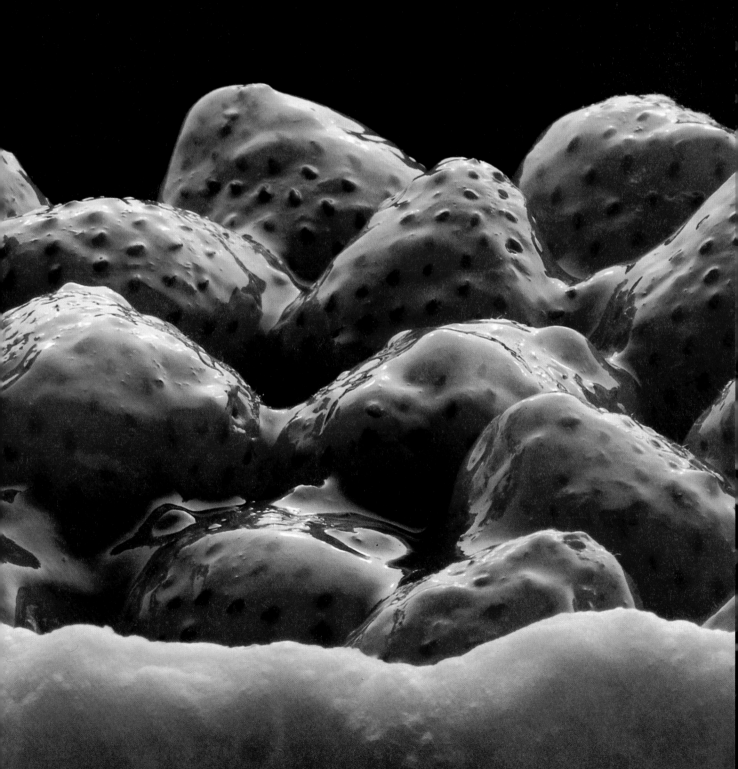

Microwave Pie Shells

Two important rules in pastry making are: work quickly and handle the dough as little as possible. Use 1½-qt. bowl for mixing because it requires fewer strokes to moisten the flour-shortening particles.

Microwave pie shells do not brown, but a few drops of food coloring in the liquid will give you a golden crust. Shells must be microwaved before filling or the crust will not cook properly.

One Crust Pastry

⅓ cup shortening
2 tablespoons butter or margarine, room temperature
1 cup all-purpose flour
½ teaspoon salt
3 tablespoons cold water
3 or 4 drops yellow food coloring, optional

Makes 8-, 9- or 10-in. pie shell

Two Crust Pastry

⅔ cup shortening
3 tablespoons butter or margarine, room temperature
2 cups all-purpose flour
1 teaspoon salt
⅓ to ½ cup cold water
7 or 8 drops yellow food coloring, optional

Divide dough in half before rolling out.

Makes 2 pie shells

How to Prepare a Pie Shell for Microwave

Cut shortening and butter into flour and salt using lowest speed of mixer or a pastry blender until particles resemble coarse crumbs or small peas.

Combine water and food coloring. Sprinkle over mixture while stirring with fork, until particles are just moist enough to cling together and form a ball. You may not need all the water.

Add just the right amount of water. Too little makes a dry dough which is hard to roll out and cracks around the edge. Too much makes a sticky dough. Either will result in tough pastry.

Flour pastry cloth evenly, working in some flour with your hands. Cloth or stocking covered rolling pin reduces amount of flour and handling needed and makes tender pastry.

Form dough into ball. Flatten to ½ in. Roll out on floured pastry cloth to scant ⅛-in. thick circle, at least 2-in. larger than inverted pie plate.

To maintain a circular shape and even thickness, roll from the center to edge in all directions.

Transfer rolled out pastry to pie plate by folding in half, then in half again; lift carefully to plate.

Unfold pastry and fit loosely into plate. Pat out air pockets on bottom. Lift sides and let fall gently into bend of plate. Do not stretch dough or it will shrink while microwaving.

Let pastry relax in plate about 10 minutes to reduce shrinkage. Then make a high standing fluted rim which will contain bubbling and make more room for the filling.

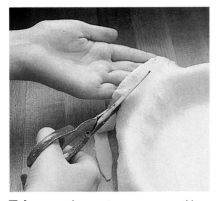

Trim overhang to generous ½-in. Fold to form standing rim. Place right index finger inside rim and left thumb and index finger on outside of rim.

Push pastry into "V" shape every ½-in. After fluting the entire rim, pinch the flutes to make sharp edges.

Prick crust with fork continuously at bend of dish, make pricks on bottom and side ½-in. apart. See special instructions on page 116 when making a custard pie.

How to Microwave a Pie Shell

Microwave at High 5 to 7 minutes, rotating dish ½ turn every 3 minutes. If crust is cooking unevenly, rotate ¼ turn every minute. If brown spot appears, cover with small piece of foil.

Watch closely. Check before minimum time. Times can vary with each crust because of differences in thickness or amount of water used. If crust bubbles, gently push back into shape.

Check for doneness by looking through bottom of glass pie plate. Crust will not brown, but will appear dry and opaque.

Pie Crust Variations

Add variety, color, flavor and texture to pie crust. Add ingredients to flour in One Crust Pastry, page 100, before cutting in shortening unless otherwise directed. Flouring pastry cloth with whole wheat flour instead of all-purpose will also add color to pastry.

Coconut Crust: Add ½ cup flaked coconut. Complements cherry, rhubarb and cream pies.

Spice Crust: Add 1 tablespoon sugar, 1 teaspoon cinnamon and ¼ teaspoon nutmeg. Use with cream, custard, pumpkin, mincemeat and apple pies.

Cheese Crust: Omit butter and add ½ cup shredded Cheddar cheese. Serve with apple, pear, chantilly pie, or main dish pies.

Coffee Crust: Add 1 to 2 teaspoons instant coffee to the water and 2 tablespoons finely chopped pecans or walnuts to the flour. Adds contrast to cream and chiffon pies.

Nut Crust: Add ¼ cup finely chopped nuts and ¼ teaspoon nutmeg. Use with cream pies, mincemeat and chiffon pies.

Chocolate Crust: Add 1 tablespoon sugar and 2 tablespoons cocoa. (Or ¼ cup cocoa mix). Serve with chocolate chiffon and cream pies.

Commercial Pie Crust Mix

Herb Crust: Add ¼ teaspoon garlic powder and 1 teaspoon mixed herbs (oregano, thyme, marjoram, parsley, etc.) Use for main dishes and appetizers.

Whole Wheat Crust: Substitute whole wheat flour for all-purpose flour. Accents cream, chiffon, mincemeat, apple and other fruit pies.

Prepare as directed on label adding 3 or 4 drops yellow food color to water before mixing. Roll out and microwave as directed for One Crust Pastry, page 100.

Pastry Cut Outs

Traditional 2 crust pies cannot be baked in a microwave oven, but Pastry Cut Outs give microwaved fruit pies the appearance of a top crust. The decorative shapes contrast with colorful fruit fillings for eye and appetite appeal.

When making pie crust, you will always have leftover dough pieces. Use these leftovers to make Pastry Cut Outs.

Roll out leftover pastry pieces to ⅛-in. thickness (no thinner). Cut into 6 pieces with cookie cutter. Sprinkle with a mixture of 1 teaspoon sugar and ⅛ teaspoon cinnamon, then arrange in circle on pie plate, microwave baking sheet or wax paper.

Always sprinkle sugar on pastry before transferring to dish. Loose sugar on dish may burn. Sugar can also be sprinkled on Cut Outs after microwaving.

Rolled out dough may also be cut into a 6- or 7-in. circle. Prick top to outline 6 wedges. Microwave Cut Outs or circles as directed below. Arrange on fruit pie before serving.

How to Microwave Pastry Cut Outs

Cut dough in 6 pieces with cookie cutter, or make one 6- or 7-in. circle and prick with fork to mark 6 wedges. Sprinkle with sugar and cinnamon; transfer to wax paper.

Arrange cookie shapes in ring. Microwave at High 2 to 4 minutes until dry and puffy, rotating every minute. Watch closely.

Make lattice top with 1½ recipes of One Crust Pastry. Roll pastry to 8-in. circle on wax paper, cut in 6 or 8 1-in. wide strips. Microwave as directed. Loosen from wax paper while warm.

103

Double Crust Pies with Toppings

This is as close to a two crust pie as you can come in the microwave oven. Part of the crust is reserved to sprinkle over the top while the other half is used to make a pie shell which is microwaved before filling.

Crumble Pastry

2 cups all-purpose flour
1 teaspoon salt
⅔ cup shortening
3 tablespoons butter or
    margarine
⅓ cup cold water
6 or 7 drops yellow food coloring

    Makes 1 double crust pastry

How to Microwave Crumble Pastry

Place in large mixing bowl flour, salt, shortening and butter. Mix on lowest speed of mixer or with pastry blender until particles resemble coarse crumbs.

Remove 1½ cups mixture to pie plate. Combine water and food coloring. Sprinkle 2 tablespoons over crumbs in plate, tossing with fork until well mixed but crumbly.

Spread over bottom of plate. Microwave at High 4 to 6 minutes. Cool and crumble finely. Set aside.

Sprinkle water over mixture in bowl, while stirring with fork, just until moist. Roll out; fit into pie plate and microwave crust as directed on page 101.

Prepare fruit or other filling as directed in recipe for a Crumble Crust Pie, page 106. Spread filling in cooked shell.

Sprinkle with reserved crumbs. Microwave as directed in recipe for filling selected.

French Streusel Pastry

½ cup shortening
2 tablespoons butter or
  margarine, room
  temperature
1½ cups all-purpose flour
½ teaspoon salt

2 to 3 tablespoons cold water
3 or 4 drops yellow food
  coloring
2 tablespoons brown or
  granulated sugar
½ teaspoon cinnamon

Makes 9- or 10-in. pastry shell

Cut shortening and butter into flour and salt with pastry blender or at low speed of mixer, until particles resemble coarse crumbs. Reserve 1 cup.

Combine water and food coloring. Sprinkle over flour mixture while stirring with fork, until dough is moist enough to hold together.

Roll out, fit into pie plate and microwave as directed on page 101.

Combine reserved crumbs, sugar and cinnamon. Sprinkle on top of fillings and microwave as directed in recipe.

Butter Crumb Pastry Topping

1 cup all-purpose flour
¼ cup plus 2 tablespoons butter
  or margarine

½ teaspoon salt

Tops 1 casserole or pie,
  or 6 dumplings

Beat ingredients in small mixing bowl at low speed until particles are fine. Sprinkle on top of filling; microwave as directed in recipe.

Variation:

Quantity Mix: Increase flour to 4 cups, butter to 1½ cups (3 sticks) and salt to 2 teaspoons. Mix in a large bowl as directed. Place in container. Cover and refrigerate up to 2 months or freeze.

Graham Cracker Crust

¼ cup plus 1 tablespoon butter
  or margarine
1⅓ cups fine graham cracker or
  cereal crumbs
2 tablespoons brown or
  granulated sugar

Makes 9- or 10-in. crumb shell

Melt butter in 9- or 10-in. pie plate at High, 45 to 60 seconds. Stir in crumbs and sugar. Reserve 2 tablespoons crumb mixture for garnish, if desired.

Press crumbs firmly and evenly against bottom and side of plate. (Pressing with a smaller pie plate or custard cup works well.)

Microwave at High 1½ minutes; rotate ½ turn after 1 minute. Cool.

Variation:
Cookie Crumb Crust:
Substitute finely crushed vanilla wafers, gingersnaps or chocolate wafers for graham cracker crumbs. Decrease butter to ¼ cup and omit sugar.

Fruit Pies

Microwaved fruit pies have a marvelous fresh fruit flavor and texture because of the shorter cooking time. They also freeze well.

As with all microwaved pies, the shell must be baked before the filling is added. Follow the directions on page 101. Fruit pies bubble hard in the microwave oven. Read the directions below when filling the crust. If you are using a Crumble or Streusel Crust, sprinkle the topping over the filling before microwaving. If you make the pie in advance and wish to serve it warm, microwave single pieces 15 to 20 seconds, or a whole pie 1 to 1½ minutes.

Crumble Crust Apple Pie

1 microwaved 9- or 10-in.
  Crumble Crust Pastry,
  page 104
4 to 5 cups sliced pared apples

⅔ cup sugar
½ teaspoon cinnamon
2 tablespoons flour

Makes 9- or 10-in. pie

Combine all ingredients. Turn into shell. Sprinkle with reserved crumbs. Set pie on wax paper in oven. Microwave at High 14 to 18 minutes, or until apples are tender*, rotating ¼ turn after 6 minutes, then every 3 to 4 minutes.

Variations:

Crumble Crust Fruit Pies: Other fresh fruits may be substituted for apples. Blueberries are very juicy so use 3 to 4 cups, fresh or frozen. Omit cinnamon.

Crumble Crust Pear and Peach Pie: Substitute sliced, fresh pears or peaches for apples; and brown sugar for white.

Crumble Crust Canned Pie Filling: Substitute 1 can (21 oz.) pie filling for apples. Place filling in shell and sprinkle with reserved crumbs. Microwave 7 to 10 minutes, rotating every 4 minutes.

*If filling starts to bubble hard, reduce power to 70% (Medium-High) or 50% (Medium) and add several minutes to microwave time if needed.

How to Prepare Fruit Pies for Microwave

Measure pie plate. Some 9-in. pie plates measure a full 9-in. across the top, while others are only 8½-in. Most pie plates are 1½-in. deep, but a few dishes are only 1-in. deep.

Height of flute and amount of shrinkage during microwaving affect how much filling the baked shell will hold.

Combination Cooking

Prepare pie as directed in your conventional recipe, using a pie plate which is suitable for both microwave and conventional ovens. Set on wax paper in microwave oven. Microwave at High until fruit is almost tender and is very hot, 8 to 12 minutes, rotating after 5 minutes.

Place in a preheated 425° conventional oven. Bake 15 to 20 minutes until a rich golden brown and bubbling juice is clear near center.

Don't fill too full, as fruit pies bubble hard. When ranges of fruit are given, use the lower quantity for smaller pie plates. If your shell does not hold all the filling, bake some separately in a custard cup.

Place wax paper in oven to catch spills. If pie bubbles hard, reduce power to 70% (Medium-High) or 50% (Medium); add more time if needed.

Deep-Dish Apple Pie

1 recipe Butter Crumb Pastry
    Topping (about 2½ cups),
    page 105
5 to 6 cups sliced pared apples,
    (use lesser amount for
    9-in. pie)
¼ cup raisins, optional
¾ cup sugar
3 tablespoons flour
½ teaspoon cinnamon
¼ teaspoon nutmeg

Makes 1 large pie
(6 to 8 servings)

In large mixing bowl, combine apples and remaining ingredients. Turn into buttered 9- or 10-in. deep-dish pie plate.* Top with crumb mixture. Sprinkle with cinnamon-sugar, if desired.

Set pie on wax paper in oven. Microwave at High 11 to 16 minutes, or until apples are tender, rotating ½ turn after 6 minutes, then every 3 minutes.

*If you don't have a deep-dish pie plate, use a 9-in. (1½-qt.) round baking dish. If filling is bubbling very hard, reduce power to 70% (Medium-High) or 50% (Medium). Increase cooking time several minutes if needed.

Variations:

Deep-Dish Pear Pie: Substitute sliced fresh pears for apples and add 2 tablespoons lemon juice.

Deep-Dish Peach Pie: Substitute sliced fresh peaches for apples.

Deep-Dish Blueberry Pie: Substitute 4 to 5 cups fresh blueberries for apples.

Deep-Dish Cherry Pie: Substitute 4 to 5 cups fresh cherries for apples.

Deep-Dish Rhubarb Pie: Substitute cut-up fresh or frozen (thawed) rhubarb for apples. Increase sugar to 1½ cups and flour to ¼ cup.

Raisin Pie

1 microwaved 9-in. French
Streusel Pastry, page 105
⅓ cup granulated sugar
⅓ cup packed brown sugar
2 tablespoons cornstarch
Dash nutmeg
1 cup water
2 cups raisins
1 tablespoon grated orange
peel
¼ cup orange juice
2 tablespoons lemon juice

Makes 9-in. pie

In medium mixing bowl or 1½- or
2-qt. casserole, combine
sugars, cornstarch, nutmeg,
water and raisins. Microwave at
High 6 to 8 minutes, or until
thickened and clear, stirring
every 2 minutes. Stir in peel and
juices. Pour into shell. Sprinkle
with reserved crumbs.

Set pie on wax paper in oven.
Microwave at 50% (Medium) 6 to
9 minutes, or until bubbly in
center, rotating ½ turn every 2 or
3 minutes.

Mincemeat Apple Pie

1 microwaved 9-in. Crumble
Crust Pastry, page 104
1 package (9 oz.) condensed
mincemeat
1½ cups water
1 to 3 tablespoons sugar
2 cups chopped apples

Makes 9-in. pie

Crumble condensed mincemeat
into a 4-cup measure or small
mixing bowl; add water and
sugar. Microwave at High 5 to 6
minutes, or until mixture is
cooked. Stir in apples; cool. Turn
mixture into shell. Sprinkle with
reserved crumbs.

Set pie on wax paper in oven.
Microwave 12 to 14 minutes, or
until apples are tender and filling
appears cooked in center,
rotating ½ turn after 6 minutes,
then every 3 minutes.

Strawberry Glacé Pie

    1 microwaved 9-in. One Crust
        Pastry, page 100
    1 quart fresh strawberries
    ⅓ cup sugar
1½ tablespoons cornstarch
    1 package (10 oz.) frozen
        strawberries*, thawed,
        page 7
    1 tablespoon lemon juice

                    Makes 9-in. pie

Place washed and dried fresh strawberries in shell. In 4-cup measure or small mixing bowl, combine sugar and cornstarch. Stir in thawed strawberries. Microwave at High 3 to 8 minutes, or until thickened and clear, stirring every 2 minutes. Stir in lemon juice; cool. Spoon over fresh strawberries, spreading carefully to cover. Refrigerate several hours.

*1 cup mashed fresh strawberries may be substituted for the frozen strawberries.

Glazed Peach Pie

    1 microwaved 9-in. One Crust
        Pastry, page 100, or Graham
        Cracker Crust, page 105
    5 cups sliced, peeled, fresh
        peaches, divided
    ⅔ cup sugar
    2 tablespoons cornstarch
    ¼ cup water
    2 tablespoons lemon juice

                    Makes 9-in. pie

Mash 1 cup peach slices in blender or with fork. In 4-cup measure or small mixing bowl, combine sugar and cornstarch. Stir in water, lemon juice and mashed peaches. Microwave at High 2 to 5 minutes, or until thickened and clear, stirring after 2 minutes, then every minute. Place remaining peach slices in shell. Spoon peach glaze over peach slices, spreading carefully to cover. Refrigerate several hours. Top with whipped cream or ice cream, if desired.

Pineapple-Lemon Pie

1 microwaved 9-in. One Crust
   Pastry, page 100
1 cup sugar
¼ cup cornstarch
¼ teaspoon salt
1 cup water, divided
1 can (8 oz.) crushed pineapple
3 or 4 egg yolks, slightly beaten
1 tablespoon grated lemon peel
⅓ cup lemon juice
1 tablespoon butter or
   margarine
   Three Egg White Meringue,
   below

Makes 9-in. pie

In small mixing bowl or 1½-qt. casserole, combine sugar, cornstarch, salt and ¼ cup water. Stir in remaining water and pineapple. Microwave at High 6 to 8 minutes, or until thickened and clear, stirring every 2 or 3 minutes.

Mix a little hot mixture into egg yolks. Blend yolks into remaining pineapple mixture. Microwave at High 1 minute. Stir in peel, juice and butter. Cool slightly; pour into shell. Top with meringue; microwave as directed. Refrigerate.

Variation:

Lemon Meringue Pie: Omit pineapple and increase water to 1¾ cups.

Three Egg White Meringue

3 egg whites
1 teaspoon cornstarch
¼ teaspoon cream of tartar
6 tablespoons sugar

Makes meringue for
8- to 9-in. pie

The quantity of meringue can be changed by adding more or less egg whites. Use 2 tablespoons sugar per white. Add or decrease 1 minute microwaving for each white.

How to Microwave Three Egg White Meringue

Place in small mixing bowl egg whites, cornstarch and cream of tartar. Beat until soft mounds form. Add sugar, a tablespoon at at time, continuing to beat until straight peaks form when beaters are raised. Spread over filling, sealing to crust edge. If desired, sprinkle meringue lightly with graham cracker crumbs.

Microwave at 50% (Medium) 3 to 6 minutes until meringue is set, rotating ½ turn after half the time. If a browned meringue is desired, microwave 3 to 4 minutes. Then place under broiler 2 to 4 minutes, watching closely.

Cream Pies

Microwaving simplifies the preparation of smooth cream fillings. It eliminates constant stirring, which is needed conventionally to keep the filling from scorching and sticking to the bottom of the pan. Clean up is easy after microwaving. Cream fillings are made of milk and sugar, thickened with cornstarch or flour and enriched with egg. The filling and pie shell are microwaved separately, then combined and chilled. If the recipe calls for egg yolks alone, you may use the whites to make a meringue which is spread over the warm filling and microwaved before the pie is chilled.

How to Make Smooth Cream Fillings

Combine dry ingredients first before adding liquid.

Stir in milk gradually to make smooth mixture, starting with about ¼ cup and then increasing the amount.

Microwave at High until filling starts to boil, then stir every minute, until very thick to make sure filling is smooth and starch is cooked.

Add a little hot mixture to the beaten egg yolks (eggs) to prevent lumping or quick-cooking of the egg.

Stir blended yolk mixture into remaining milk mixture. Microwave only until it boils well, 30 to 60 seconds.

Serve cream and custard pies the day they are made. Store leftover pie in the refrigerator and use within 24 hours.

Sour Cream Raisin Pie ▶

1 microwaved 9-in. One Crust
   Pastry, page 100
¾ cup sugar
2 tablespoons flour
1 teaspoon cinnamon
¼ teaspoon salt
¼ teaspoon nutmeg
   Dash cloves
¾ cup raisins
1 cup dairy sour cream
½ cup milk
3 egg yolks
   Three Egg White Meringue,
   page 111

Makes 9-in. pie

In 4-cup measure or small
mixing bowl, combine dry ingredients and raisins. Blend in sour
cream, then milk and egg yolks
until smooth.

Microwave at High 5 to 6
minutes, or until very thick,
stirring vigorously after 2
minutes, then every minute. Beat
until smooth. Spoon into shell.
Cool slightly. Top with meringue
and microwave as directed.

Homemade Cream Pie

1 microwaved 9-in. One Crust
   Pastry, page 100, or Cookie
   Crumb Crust, page 105
   Cream Filling, page 136
   Three Egg White Meringue,
   page 111

Makes 9-in. pie

Prepare Cream Filling as
directed. Cool slightly and pour
into shell. Top with meringue and
microwave as directed. Or chill
completely and top with whipped cream just before serving.

NOTE: Cream and custard pies
should always be refrigerated.

Fruit-glazed Cream Pie ▲

1 microwaved 9-in. One Crust
   Pastry, page 100

Cream Filling
1 package (3 to 3⅝ oz.) vanilla
   pudding and pie filling mix
2 cups milk, divided

Glaze
1 package (10 oz.) frozen
   sweetened strawberries or
   other fruit, thawed and
   drained, page 7
1 tablespoon cornstarch
1 tablespoon lemon juice

Makes 9-in. pie

Place pudding mix in 4-cup measure or 1½-qt. mixing bowl. Stir in
about ⅓ cup milk until smooth. Stir in remaining milk. Microwave at
High 4 to 7 minutes, or until mixture boils, stirring after 2 minutes then
every minute. Pour into shell. Refrigerate until chilled.

In 4-cup measure or small mixing bowl, combine strawberry juice
and cornstarch. Stir in strawberries. Microwave at High 2 to 5
minutes, or until thickened and clear, stirring every minute. Stir in
lemon juice. Cool 10 minutes. Spoon over filling, spreading carefully
to cover. Refrigerate several hours.

Cream Pie Special

1 microwaved 9-in. Graham
  Cracker Crust, page 105, or
  One Crust Pastry, page 100
1 package (3 to 3⅝ oz.)
  regular pudding and pie
  filling mix (any flavor)
1½ cups milk, divided
1 egg, beaten
⅔ cup whipping cream
1 teaspoon vanilla

Makes 9-in. pie

Place pudding mix in 4-cup
measure or small mixing bowl.
Stir in about ¼ cup milk until
smooth. Stir in remaining milk.
Microwave at High 3 to 5 minutes, or until boiling. Stir after 2
minutes, then every minute.

Mix a little hot mixture into egg.
Blend egg mixture into
remaining pudding mixture.
Microwave 30 to 60 seconds; stir
well. Cover with circle of foil;
cool. Remove foil; beat well.

Beat cream and vanilla until stiff.
Fold into filling. Spoon into shell.
Sprinkle with reserved crumbs
or top with Pastry Cut Outs, page
103. Refrigerate several hours.

Chantilly Fruit Pie ▲

1 microwaved 9-in. One Crust
  Pastry, page 100
4 cups miniature marshmallows
⅓ cup milk
3 to 4 cups sliced fresh fruit or
  berries
¾ cup whipping cream
2 tablespoons sugar
1 teaspoon vanilla
¼ teaspoon mace or nutmeg,
  optional

Makes 9-in. pie

In medium mixing bowl or 2-qt.
casserole, combine marshmallows and milk. Microwave at
High 1½ to 3 minutes, or until
marshmallows are melted,
stirring every minute. Stir until
smooth. Let stand until thickened but not set. Fold in fruit.

Beat cream, sugar, vanilla and
mace until stiff. Fold into marshmallow mixture. Spoon into shell.
Refrigerate several hours.
Garnish with fruit as desired.

Creamy Lemon Cheese Pie

1 microwaved One Crust
  Pastry, page 100
1 package (8 oz.) cream
  cheese
2 eggs
½ cup sugar
2 teaspoons grated lemon peel
2 tablespoons lemon juice
2 tablespoons milk

Makes 9-in. pie

Microwave cream cheese in
small mixing bowl at 50%
(Medium) 1 minute to soften.
Beat until fluffy. Add eggs; beat
well. Blend in remaining
ingredients. Microwave at 50%
(Medium) 3 to 4½ minutes, or
until heated, stirring well every 2
minutes. Turn into shell.

Microwave at 50% (Medium) 6 to
10 minutes, or until almost set in
center, rotating ¼ turn every 3
minutes. Chill before serving.

◄ Key Lime Pie

1 microwaved 9-in. Graham Cracker Crust, page 105, or One Crust Pastry, page 100
1 can (14 oz.) sweetened condensed milk
3 egg yolks
2 teaspoons grated lime peel, optional
½ cup lime juice
2 or 3 drops green food coloring, optional
Three Egg White Meringue, page 111

Makes 9-in. pie

Blend milk and egg yolks, at low speed. Add peel, juice and coloring; blend until smooth. Pour into shell. Top with meringue; microwave as directed. Refrigerate several hours.

Swiss Fudge Pie ►

1 microwaved 9-in. One Crust Pastry, page 100
1 can (14 oz.) sweetened condensed milk
1 cup (6 oz.) chocolate chips
⅓ cup almond slices

Makes 9-in. pie

How to Microwave Swiss Fudge Pie

Prepare and microwave pastry shell. Set aside. In 4-cup measure, microwave milk at High 1 to 1½ minutes, or until hot.

Stir in chocolate chips until melted. Microwave at High 20 to 45 seconds if needed to melt chips. Pour into pie shell.

Microwave at High 3 minutes. Sprinkle with almonds. Microwave at 50% (Medium) 1 to 4 minutes, or until cooked in center. Cool before serving.

Custard Pies

Custard pies are one crust pies with the filling baked in the crust. The filling is usually very thin, so it is important to seal the prick holes or bake a crust with fewer pricks. Because they are made with eggs, custard pies should be eaten the day they are baked. Store leftover pie in the refrigerator, and use within 24 hours.

2 Ways to Prepare Crust for Pies with Liquid Fillings.

Method 1. Prepare and microwave shell as directed on page 101. Brush crust with lightly beaten egg yolk to seal holes. Microwave at High 30 to 60 seconds until yolk is set.

Method 2. Make 6 pricks in bend of plate, 6 on bottom and 6 on sides. Microwave at High 3 minutes, checking every minute and pushing bubbles back against plate. Fill shell with 1 pound navy beans. Microwave 3 minutes. Cool a few minutes. Carefully remove beans; save for another time. If crust does not appear dry, microwave 1 to 2 minutes.

How to Microwave Custard Pie

Microwave filling in mixing bowl at 50% (Medium) until very hot, stirring with wire whisk as directed in recipe.

Fill shell as full as you can without spilling over top. Bake any leftover filling in custard cup after pie is done.

Place pie on inverted saucer in oven. Microwave at 50% (Medium) until set around edges and almost set in center, rotating ¼ turn every 3 or 4 minutes.

Touch center gently. When done, filling should be almost firm in center.

Let cool or set before serving. Custard continues to cook as it cools. Overcooking causes filling to "weep" or become watery.

Warm pie, if desired, for 1 to 1½ minutes at 50% (Medium). Microwave single pieces 15 to 20 seconds.

Custard Pie

1 microwaved 9-in. One Crust
  Pastry, page 100*
4 eggs
⅔ cup sugar
2 teaspoons cornstarch
1¾ cups milk, scalded in
  microwave oven
1 teaspoon vanilla
¼ teaspoon salt
¼ teaspoon nutmeg

Makes 9-in. pie

Blend eggs in medium mixing
bowl or 1½-qt. casserole at low
speed. Blend sugar and
cornstarch, add to eggs. Mix in
remaining ingredients.
Microwave at 50% (Medium) 3 to
6 minutes, or until mixture is very
hot, stirring every 2 minutes.
Pour into shell.

Set pie on inverted saucer in
oven. Microwave at 50%
(Medium) 4 to 15 minutes, or until
set around edges and almost set
in center, rotating ¼ turn every 3
minutes. Cool completely.

*See 2 Ways to Prepare Crust for
Pies with Liquid Fillings, opposite.

Pumpkin Pie ▲

9-inch

1 microwaved 9-in. One
  Crust Pastry, page 100
3 eggs, divided
1 cup canned pumpkin
½ cup packed brown sugar
1⅓ cups evaporated milk
1 tablespoon flour
1 teaspoon cinnamon
¼ teaspoon salt
¼ teaspoon ginger
¼ teaspoon nutmeg

10-inch

1 microwaved 10-in. One
  Crust Pastry, page 100
3 eggs, divided
2 cups canned pumpkin
⅔ cup packed brown sugar
1⅔ cups evaporated milk
1 tablespoon flour
1½ teaspoons cinnamon
¼ teaspoon salt
¼ teaspoon ginger
¼ teaspoon nutmeg

Makes 9- or 10-in. pie

Blend 1 egg yolk in medium mixing bowl or 2-qt. casserole at low
speed. Reserve the white. With soft brush, coat the shell with some
beaten yolk to seal holes. Microwave at High 30 to 60 seconds, or
until yolk is set.

Add 2 eggs and remaining ingredients, except the egg white, to
leftover beaten yolk. Blend well at low speed. Beat white until soft
mounds form. Stir into pumpkin mixture.

Microwave at High 3 minutes, stirring after 1½ minutes. Reduce
power to 50% (Medium). Microwave 6 to 9 minutes, or until mixture is
very hot and slightly thickened, stirring with wire whisk after 2 minutes,
then every minute. Pour into shell. Fill to about ¼ in. of top flute. Set pie
on wax paper in oven. Microwave at 50% (Medium) 11 to 26 minutes
for 9-in. pie, 14 to 33 minutes for 10-in. or 9-in. deep-dish pie, or until
set in center, rotating ¼ turn every 4 minutes. Cool completely.

Chiffon Pies

The light, fluffy filling of chiffon pies can be made in two ways. The old-fashioned type is thickened with gelatin, into which beaten egg whites and cream are folded. Today's quick chiffon pies are thickend with melted marshmallows. The gelatin or marshmallow mixture should be cooled or chilled until it mounds when dropped from a spoon. After the beaten egg whites and/or whipped cream are folded in, it should still mound. If it doesn't, chill longer before spooning into the pie shell. Use a large spoon so the pie looks light and fluffy. Chill the finished pie until firm enough to hold its shape when cut, at least 2 hours.

Short-cut Lemon Chiffon Pie

1 microwaved 9-in. Cookie Crumb Crust, page 105
4 cups miniature marshmallows or 40 large marshmallows
½ cup sugar
¼ cup milk
1 tablespoon grated lemon peel
⅓ cup lemon juice
3 to 4 drops yellow food coloring, optional
1 cup whipping cream*

Makes 9-in. pie

In medium mixing bowl or 2-qt. casserole, combine marshmallows, sugar and milk. Microwave at High 2 to 3 minutes, until marshmallows are melted, stirring every minute. Stir in peel, juice and coloring. Let stand until thickened but not set.

Beat cream until stiff. Fold into marshmallow mixture. Spoon into shell. Refrigerate several hours.

*2 cups frozen whipped topping may be substituted for cream.

Variations:

Short-cut Lime Chiffon Pie: Substitute lime juice and peel for lemon. Use green food coloring.

Short-cut Grasshopper Pie: Decrease sugar to ⅓ cup. Substitute cream de menthe syrup for peel and juice. Use green food coloring.

Short-cut Orange Chiffon Pie: Decrease sugar to ¼ cup. Use 1 tablespoon each lemon and orange peel and ¼ cup orange juice. Use 4 drops yellow and 1 small drop red coloring.

Pumpkin Chiffon Pie ▶

1 microwaved 9-in. One Crust Pastry, page 100, or Cookie Crumb Crust, page 105
1 cup canned pumpkin
½ cup packed brown sugar
¼ cup milk
1 teaspoon cinnamon
½ teaspoon nutmeg
¼ teaspoon salt
4 cups miniature marshmallows or 40 large marshmallows
1 tablespoon grated orange peel, optional
1 cup whipping cream

Makes 9-in. pie

Combine all ingredients except cream in medium mixing bowl or 2-qt. casserole. Microwave at High 2 to 6 minutes, or until marshmallows are melted, stirring every minute. Let stand until thickened but not set.

Beat cream until stiff. Fold into pumpkin mixture. Spoon into shell. Refrigerate several hours.

How to Prepare Quick Chiffon Fillings

Melt marshmallows with milk and sugar at High 2 to 3 minutes, stirring every minute.

Cool until thick but not set. Mixture should mound when dropped from a spoon.

Fold in stiffly beaten whipping cream. Mixture should still mound. If necessary, chill before spooning into microwaved shell.

◄ Old-fashioned Lemon Chiffon Pie

  1 microwaved 9-in. One Crust
     Pastry, page 100, or Cookie
     Crumb Crust, page 105
¾ cup sugar, divided
  1 envelope unflavored gelatin
¼ teaspoon salt
¼ cup water
  3 eggs, separated
  1 tablespoon grated lemon peel
⅓ cup lemon juice
  1 cup whipping cream

Makes 9-in. pie

In medium mixing bowl or 2-qt. casserole, combine ½ cup sugar, gelatin and salt. Stir in water, slightly beaten yolks, peel and juice. Microwave at 50% (Medium) 2 to 4 minutes, or until mixture is hot, stirring every minute. Let stand until thickened but not set.

Beat egg whites until soft mounds form. Gradually add ¼ cup sugar; beat until soft peaks form when beaters are raised.

Beat cream until stiff. Fold into gelatin mixture, then fold in egg whites. Spoon into shell. Refrigerate several hours.

Special Pies

These pies are slightly different and don't fit into any of the standard categories. The fillings are baked in the crust like custard pies. If the filling is thin, see 2 Ways to Prepare Crusts for Pies with Liquid Fillings, page 116.

Shoofly Pie

    1 microwaved 9- or 10-in. One
        Crust Pastry, page 100*
1¼ cups all-purpose flour
    ½ cup packed brown sugar
     1 teaspoon cinnamon
    ¼ teaspoon salt
    ¼ teaspoon nutmeg
    ¼ teaspoon ginger
     6 tablespoons butter,
        margarine or other
        shortening
    ¾ cup water
    ⅓ cup light molasses
     1 teaspoon soda

                Makes 9- or 10-in. pie

*See 2 Ways to Prepare Crust for Pies with Liquid Fillings, page 116.

NOTE: For 10-in. pie increase water to 1 cup and molasses to ½ cup.

How to Microwave Shoofly Pie

Combine flour, sugar, spices and butter until particles are fine, using medium bowl and slow speed of mixer. In 2-cup measure, microwave water at High until boiling, 1½ to 2½ minutes. Stir in molasses and soda.

Alternate layers of ⅓ crumb mixture and ½ water mixture in pastry shell, beginning and ending with crumb mixture.

Microwave at 50% (Medium) 5 minutes. Rotate ½ turn. Microwave at High 4 to 7 minutes, or until center is dry on top and springs back when touched.

Pecan Pie

1 microwaved 9-in. One Crust
    Pastry, page 100
3 eggs, divided
½ cup packed brown sugar
1 cup dark or light corn syrup
2 tablespoons butter or
    margarine, melted
1 tablespoon flour
1 teaspoon vanilla
¼ teaspoon salt
¾ to 1 cup (3 to 4 oz.) broken
    pecans

Makes 9-in. pie

Beat 1 egg yolk until blended.
With soft brush, coat the crust
with some beaten yolk to seal
holes. Microwave at High 30 to
60 seconds, or until yolk is set.

In medium mixing bowl, combine remaining eggs and white
with leftover beaten yolk. Add remaining ingredients except pecans. Blend well. Stir in pecans.
Microwave 4 minutes, stirring
after 2 minutes. Pour into shell.

Reduce power to 50% (Medium). Microwave 9 to 13 minutes,
or until filling is almost set,
rotating ¼ turn every 3 minutes.

Brownie Sundae Pie

1 microwaved 10-in. One Crust
    Pastry, page 100*
⅔ cup all-purpose flour
¼ cup shortening
1 envelope pre-melted
    unsweetened chocolate or
    1 square (1 oz.)
    unsweetened chocolate,
    melted as directed on page 7

½ cup sugar
½ teaspoon soda
½ teaspoon salt
½ teaspoon vanilla
1 egg
½ cup milk
½ cup chocolate syrup
    Confectioners' sugar

Makes 10-in. pie

Blend all ingredients except chocolate syrup and confectioners'
sugar in small mixing bowl at low speed until smooth. Beat at medium
speed 2 minutes. Turn into shell. Drizzle chocolate syrup over top.

Microwave at 50% (Medium) 7 to 9 minutes, or until top is firm,
rotating ½ turn after 3 minutes, then every 2 minutes. Sprinkle with
confectioners' sugar. Serve warm or cold, as is, or with whipped
cream or ice cream.

*See 2 Ways to Prepare Crust for Pies with Liquid Fillings, page 116.

121

Desserts

Cake Desserts

Cake desserts have a cake-like texture when baked, or are dressed-up versions of a basic cake. Most of them are make-ahead desserts. Those which are best warm can be mixed in advance and microwaved during the meal, or made early and reheated. Allow 10 to 15 seconds per serving, and reheat only the amount needed.

As with any cooking or baking, good measuring and mixing techniques are important for desserts. Read pages 4 to 7 before you start.

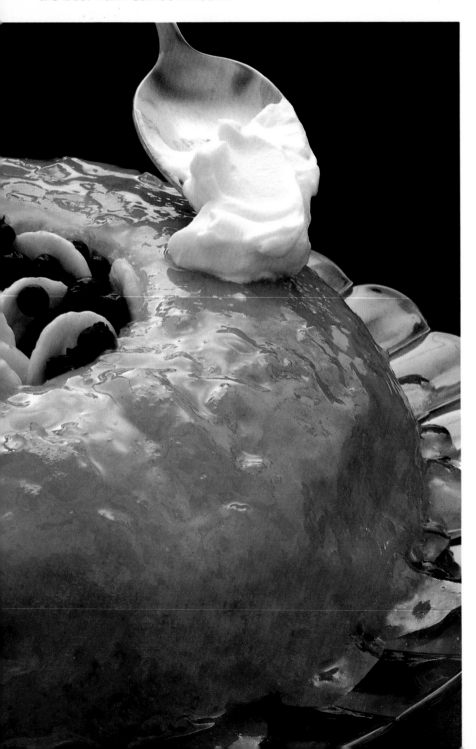

Apricot Cake 'n Fruit Ring

 1 recipe one-layer cake (Whole Egg Yellow or White, page 61)
⅓ cup apricot preserves
 1 tablespoon lemon juice
 1 pint strawberries, sliced*
 2 large bananas, sliced*
½ cup whipping cream, whipped

Makes 9 to 10 servings

Grease 2-qt. round casserole. Coat with graham cracker crumbs. Grease pint jar or similar jar and sprinkle with crumbs. Place jar, open-end up, in center of casserole. Spoon batter around jar; spread carefully. Microwave at 50% (Medium) 6 minutes, or until done, rotating ¼ turn every 3 minutes. (Cake may be done at this time.) Increase power to High. Microwave 1 to 5 minutes, if necessary. Sprinkle top with graham cracker crumbs. Cool 5 to 10 mintues. Loosen edges well and turn out onto serving plate.

Combine preserves and lemon juice. Microwave at High 15 seconds; blend well. Spread over cake. At serving time, fill center with fruit and garnish top with whipped cream. Serve with additional fruit.

*4- to 5-cup combinations of fresh fruits, such as blueberries and peaches, blueberries and bananas or raspberries and peaches may be substituted.

Boston Cream Pie

1 round layer Whole Egg Yellow
     Cake, page 61*
1 recipe Vanilla Cream Filling,
     page 71
1 recipe Chocolate Frosting,
     page 70

Makes 8 to 10 servings

Sprinkle top of hot cake with
graham cracker crumbs. Cool
cake 5 to 15 minutes; remove
from dish. Sprinkle bottom with
graham cracker crumbs. Slice
cooled cake layer horizontally to
make 2 thin layers. Place bottom
layer on cake plate. Spread with
Filling. Top with second layer.
Frost, allowing frosting to drizzle
down side. Refrigerate until
serving time.

*Line bottom of dish with 2
circles of wax paper before filling with batter for easy removal.

Gingerbread

1¼ cups all-purpose flour
  ⅓ cup packed brown sugar
  ½ teaspoon soda
  ½ teaspoon salt
  ½ teaspoon cinnamon
  ½ teaspoon ginger
  ¼ teaspoon cloves
  ⅓ cup shortening
   2 eggs
  ⅓ cup light molasses
  ¼ cup hot water

Makes 9 servings

Place all ingredients in mixing
bowl. Blend at low speed, then
beat at medium speed 2
minutes. Spread in 8×8-in.
baking dish. Shield corners of
dish with triangles of foil.

Microwave at 50% (Medium) 6
minutes, rotating ¼ turn every 3
minutes. Remove foil. Increase
power to High. Microwave 1 to
4½ minutes, or until done. Cool
directly on countertop 5 to 10
minutes. Serve warm, topped
with whipped cream, lemon
sauce or another complementary sauce, pages 144 to 147.

Pineapple Upside-down Cake

Topping:

¼ cup butter or margarine
½ cup packed brown sugar
7 to 9 pineapple rings or peach halves
  Well-drained maraschino cherries and/or pecan halves, optional
1 recipe one-layer cake (Whole Egg Yellow or White, page 61)

Makes 9 servings

How to Microwave Pineapple Upside-down Cake

Microwave butter in 8×8-in. baking dish at High 1 to 1½ minutes; spread evenly over bottom. Sprinkle with sugar.

Top with pineapple, cutting to fit as necessary. Garnish with cherries and/or pecans.

Place dish on inverted saucer in microwave oven. Microwave at High 4 minutes. Spoon cake batter evenly over fruit.

Place dish on saucer in oven. Microwave at 50% (Medium) 6 minutes, rotating ¼ turn every 3 minutes. Increase power to High.

Microwave 2½ to 8 minutes, or until top springs back or appears baked. Sprinkle with graham cracker crumbs.

Cool directly on countertop 5 minutes. Loosen edges well and turn out onto plate. Serve warm, plain or with whipped cream.

Orange Baba Desserts

1 recipe two-layer cake,
  (Whole Egg Yellow or White,
  page 61) or 1 package cake
  mix, with or without pudding
  (yellow, orange or white)
2 tablespoons shredded
  orange peel, divided
14 to 18 (7 oz.) paper drink cups
1 cup whipping cream,
  whipped or 2 cups whipped
  cream substitute

  Makes 14 to 18 servings

Orange Sauce:
½ cup butter or margarine
½ cup sugar
 2 teaspoons cornstarch
½ cup orange juice
 1 cup water
 2 tablespoons lemon juice

In 4-cup measure or 1½-qt.
mixing bowl, combine butter,
sugar, cornstarch, orange juice
and water. Microwave at High 4
to 6 minutes, or until mixture
comes to full boil, stirring after 3
minutes. Stir in lemon juice.
(Reheat, if necessary, to spoon
on cakes.)

How to Microwave Orange Baba Desserts

Prepare cake batter as directed,
adding 1 tablespoon orange peel
before mixing. Fill paper cups ⅓
to ½ full. Arrange 6 to 8 cups in
ring in microwave oven; leave at
least ½-in. between cups.

Microwave at High 2 to 4½
minutes, or until almost dry on
top, rotating cups every minute.
Let stand about 1 minute; loosen
edges carefully with small spatula and remove. Place upside-
down in large, flat dish.

Spoon hot Orange Sauce, over
cakes about 1 hour before
serving, and let stand in sauce.
Just before serving, top with
whipped cream and garnish with
shredded orange peel.

Plantation Dessert

1½ cups all-purpose flour
  1 cup sugar
  ½ cup chopped pecans or
     walnuts
  ½ teaspoon cinnamon
  ¼ teaspoon salt
  ¼ teaspoon ginger
     Dash cloves
  ¼ cup plus 2 tablespoons
     butter or margarine
  ¾ cup boiling water
  ⅓ cup light molasses
1½ teaspoons soda
     Whipped Cheese Topping,
     below
     Lemon or Orange Sauce,
     page 146

Makes 8 or 9 servings

Whipped Cheese Topping:
  1 pkg. (3 oz.) cream cheese,
     room temperature
  3 tablespoons confectioners'
     sugar
  ½ teaspoon vanilla
  ½ cup whipping cream

In small mixing bowl, beat cream cheese, sugar and vanilla. Add cream gradually, beating until very thick. Refrigerate until serving time.

How to Microwave Plantation Dessert

Combine flour, sugar, pecans, cinnamon, salt, ginger and cloves, in mixing bowl. Cut in butter until particles resemble coarse crumbs. Press 2 cups crumbly mixture in bottom of 10×6-, 8×8- or 9-in. round baking dish.

Combine water, molasses and soda; blend well. Pour over crumbly mixture in dish. Sprinkle with remaining crumbly mixture. Place dish on inverted saucer in microwave oven. Microwave at 50% (Medium) 6 minutes; rotate ¼ turn every 2 or 3 minutes.

Increase power to High. Microwave 2 to 6 minutes, or until top springs back when touched here and there, rotating ¼ turn every minute. Cool directly on countertop 10 minutes. Serve warm topped with cheese topping and sauce.

Date Torte

¾ cup all-purpose flour
¼ cup shortening
½ cup packed brown sugar
½ teaspoon soda
½ teaspoon salt
½ teaspoon vanilla
 2 eggs
½ cup dates, cut fine
½ cup dairy sour cream
 2 tablespoons water
¼ cup chopped nuts, optional

Topping:

 2 tablespoons brown sugar
 2 tablespoons dairy sour cream
¾ cup whipping cream,
    whipped and sweetened, or
    1½ cups whipped cream
    substitute

Makes 9 servings

Variations:

Nut Torte: Omit dates and increase nuts to ¾ cup.

Coconut Torte: Omit dates and add 1 cup flaked coconut.

How to Microwave Date Torte

Place all ingredients except topping in small mixing bowl. Blend at low speed, then beat at medium speed 2 minutes. Spread in 8×8-in. baking dish. Shield corners of dish with triangles of foil. Place dish on inverted saucer in oven.

Microwave at 50% (Medium) 6 minutes, rotating ¼ turn every 3 minutes. Remove foil. Increase power to High. Microwave 2 to 7 minutes, or until done. Cool directly on countertop.

Combine brown sugar and sour cream in small dish. Microwave at 50% (Medium) 30 seconds, or just until hot and sugar is melted. Stir well; cool. Spread whipped cream over torte. Drizzle with topping. Refrigerate at least 2 hours before serving.

Crisps, Cobblers & Shortcakes

These fruit desserts are topped, layered or enclosed in a baked product made with flour. It may be a streusel-like topping, pastry, cake or muffins.

Cherry Cobbler

    1 can (21 oz.) cherry or apple
        pie filling
 ¾ cup all-purpose flour
    3 tablespoons sugar, divided
 1½ teaspoons baking powder
 ¼ teaspoon salt
    2 tablespoons milk
    1 egg, slightly beaten
    2 tablespoons butter or
        margarine, melted
 ¼ cup graham cracker crumbs
 ½ teaspoon cinnamon

    Makes one 9- or 10-in. pie

How to Microwave Cherry Cobbler

Spread pie filling in 10-in. pie plate or 9-in. round baking dish. Cover; microwave at High 3 to 5 minutes, or until hot and bubbly all over, stirring after 3 minutes.

Combine flour, 2 tablespoons sugar, baking powder and salt, in mixing bowl. Combine milk, egg and butter; add to dry ingredients. Mix only until moistened. Combine crumbs, 1 tablespoon sugar and cinnamon.

Divide dough into 6 equal parts. With spoon, drop each part into crumbs; roll to coat. Arrange around edge of hot cherries. Microwave uncovered 3 to 5 minutes, or until biscuits are done, rotating ½ turn after half the time. Serve warm with cream.

Apple Brown Betty

5 cups sliced pared apples*
¾ cup packed brown sugar
½ cup raisins or cut-up dates
1 teaspoon cinnamon
¼ teaspoon salt
¼ cup butter or margarine, melted
3 cups small dry bread cubes or coarse crumbs
½ cup water

Makes 6 to 8 servings

Combine apples, sugar, raisins, cinnamon and salt; set aside. Toss butter and bread cubes. Layer half the apple mixture in 2-qt. casserole; top with half the bread cubes. Repeat with remaining apple mixture and bread cubes. Pour water over bread cubes; cover.

Microwave at High 8 minutes, rotating ¼ turn every 4 minutes. Microwave uncovered 6 to 10 minutes, or until apples are tender, rotating ¼ turn every 4 minutes. Serve warm with Lemon Butter Sauce, page 146, or cream.

*Peaches, pears or rhubarb may be substituted for apples. For rhubarb, substitute 1⅓ cups granulated sugar for brown.

Apple Cheese Crisp

¼ cup plus 1 tablespoon butter or margarine
½ cup packed brown sugar
¾ cup quick-cooking rolled oats
¾ cup all-purpose flour
6 cups sliced pared apples
1 tablespoon lemon juice
⅓ cup granulated sugar
3 tablespoons flour, divided
½ teaspoon cinnamon
¼ teaspoon salt
3 or 4 ounces cream cheese, room temperature
1 tablespoon milk
¼ cup granulated sugar
1 egg

Makes 9 servings

Microwave butter in casserole at High 45 to 60 seconds, or until melted. Stir in brown sugar and oats. Microwave at High 2 minutes. Stir in ¾ cup flour; set aside.

Combine apples, juice, ⅓ cup sugar, 2 tablespoons flour, cinnamon and salt in 8×8-in. baking dish. Stir and spread evenly. Microwave at High 8 minutes, stirring after half the time.

Blend cream cheese, milk, sugar, egg and 1 tablespoon flour. Pour evenly over apples. Sprinkle with crumbly mixture. Microwave at High 6 to 10 minutes, or until apples are tender, rotating ½ turn after half the time. Serve warm or cold, plain or topped with whipped cream.

◄ Apple Dumpling Cups

6 small (2 to 2½-in.) apples, pared, quartered and cored
6 tablespoons raisins
6 to 9 tablespoons brown sugar Cinnamon
3 teaspoons butter or margarine, if desired
1 recipe Butter Crumb Pastry Topping, page 105

Makes 6 servings

Place 1 apple (4 quarters) in each of six 5- or 6-oz. custard cups, individual souffle or casserole dishes. Top with 1 tablespoon raisins, 1 to 1½ tablespoons brown sugar, dash cinnamon and ½ teaspoon butter. Place about ¼ cup topping on top. Place cups in ring on wax paper in oven. Microwave at High 7 to 10 minutes, or until apples are tender, rearranging and rotating cups every 3 minutes.

NOTE: One or two desserts can be made. Refrigerate remaining crumb topping and make more desserts as desired. For each dessert, microwave 1½ to 2½ minutes. Rotate cups after half the time when baking 2 or more.

Variation:

Pear or Peach Dumpling Cups: Small pears or small peaches may be substituted for apples.

Southern Nut Baskets

24 cupcake liners
¼ cup butter or magarine
1 cup graham cracker crumbs
2 tablespoons sugar

Filling:

⅔ cup chopped pecans or walnuts
3 eggs
½ cup light or dark corn syrup
⅓ cup packed brown sugar
2 tablespoons butter or margarine, melted
1 tablespoon flour
1 teaspoon vanilla

Makes 12 servings

Place 2 liners in each of twelve 5- or 6-oz. custard cups. In small bowl, microwave butter at High 45 to 60 seconds, or until melted. Stir in crumbs and sugar. Place rounded tablespoonful of crumb mixture in each liner. Press down firmly with bottom of small glass.

Place a scant tablespoon of pecans in each cup. Blend remaining filling ingredients; place 2 tablespoons in each cup. Arrange 6 cups in circle in oven. Microwave at High 2 to 4 minutes, or until mixture bubbles in spots and tops are quite firm, rotating and rearranging cups every minute. Remove desserts as they appear done. Cool. Serve topped with whipped cream.

NOTE: If necessary to re-use custard cups for remaining desserts, cool 2 to 3 minutes, then transfer desserts to paper towel.

Swedish Apple Torte

1½ tablespoons sugar
¼ teaspoon cinnamon
½ cup butter or margarine
½ cup shortening
3 cups all-purpose flour
1 teaspoon salt
1 egg, beaten
¼ cup whipping cream
5 or 6 drops yellow food
    coloring
1 can (1 lb.) applesauce
½ cup whipping cream,
    whipped, or 1 cup whipped
    cream substitute

Serves 8

How to Microwave Swedish Apple Torte

Combine sugar and cinnamon; set aside. Cut butter and shortening into flour and salt at low speed or with pastry blender until particles resemble coarse crumbs.

Combine egg, cream and coloring. Sprinkle over flour mixture while stirring with fork until dough is just moist enough to hold together. If necessary, add a few more drops cream.

Form dough into ball. Divide into 4 equal parts. Roll out 1 part at a time on floured pastry cloth or wax paper to 10-in. circle. Use pie plate for guide in cutting circle.

Sprinkle with 1 teaspoon sugar mixture. Cut out a 2½- to 3-in. circle in center. Reserve circle. Transfer ring to baking dish or pie plate lined with wax paper.

Microwave at High 4 to 6 minutes, or until pastry appears dry and opaque. Rotate ¼ turn after 2 minutes, then every 30 seconds. Watch closely. Repeat with remaining pastry. Cut small circles in half. Microwave 1½ to 3 minutes.

Place 1 ring on serving plate, thirty minutes before serving. Top with ⅓ of the applesauce. Continue to stack rings and applesauce, leaving top plain. Refrigerate. Garnish with whipped cream and small half circles before serving.

Fruit Desserts

Fruit desserts are refreshing, nutritious and low in calories. Because of its speed, microwaving enhances the fresh flavor and texture of fruits.

Fruits microwave quickly, and continue to cook a few minutes after removal from the oven. They should be just fork-tender with a slightly firm, fresh texture.

While fresh fruits are available all year 'round, most of them have peak seasons when their quality and price are best. Fruits in season are naturally sweet and need little or no additional sugar.

Some fruits turn brown when peeled and sliced. Prepare them just before serving time, or sprinkle them with lemon juice.

Bananas Royale ▲

3 or 4 medium bananas, peeled*
2 tablespoons butter or margarine
¼ cup packed brown sugar
¼ teaspoon nutmeg
¼ teaspoon cinnamon
¼ cup whipping cream
1 teaspoon rum flavoring or 2 tablespoons rum
  Ice cream

Makes 6 servings

Slice bananas in half lengthwise, then crosswise once. Place butter in 2-qt. casserole. Microwave at High about 30 seconds, or until melted. Stir in sugar, spices and cream. Microwave at High 1½ to 2 minutes, or until slightly thickened; blend well. Add bananas, turning to coat with sauce. Microwave at High 30 seconds. Stir in rum. Serve immediately over ice cream. (To flame, omit rum and follow directions on page 7.)

*Bananas should be very firm and slightly green. If too ripe, they cook to pieces very quickly.

Cherries Jubilee

1 can (16 oz.) pitted dark sweet cherries*
¼ cup sugar
2 teaspoons cornstarch
1 quart vanilla ice cream

Makes 6 to 8 servings

Drain cherries, reserving juice. In 1½-qt. casserole or microwave-proof serving bowl, combine sugar and cornstarch. Gradually stir in cherry juice. Microwave at High 2 to 4 minutes, or until clear and slightly thickened, stirring every minute. Stir in cherries. Microwave at High 30 seconds. Serve hot over ice cream.

*For less sauce, use ¼ cup cherry juice and decrease sugar to 3 tablespoons and cornstarch to 1 teaspoon. Microwave 1 to 1½ minutes.

NOTE: For flaming Cherries Jubilee, see page 7.

Peaches & Sour Cream

1 can (29 oz.) peach halves,
    drained
4 to 6 tablespoons brown sugar
    Cinnamon
1 cup dairy sour cream
    Nutmeg

Make 5 or 6 servings

Place peaches around edge of
large pie plate or 9-in. round
baking dish. Place ½ tablespoon sugar in center of each.
Sprinkle with cinnamon. Microwave at High 3 to 6 minutes, or
until sugar bubbles, rotating ¼
turn every minute. Top each half
with spoonful of sour cream.
Sprinkle with nutmeg.
Refrigerate at least 8 hours or
overnight, covering after cool.

Chocolate Bananas

10 wooden skewers
 5 firm bananas, peeled and
    halved crosswise
 1 cup chocolate chips
 3 tablespoons shortening

Makes 10 servings

Insert skewers in cut ends of
bananas. Freeze at least 2
hours. Just before serving, place
chips and shortening in small
mixing bowl. Microwave at 50%
(Medium) 2½ to 4 minutes, or
until most of the chips are shiny
and soft; blend well. Dip frozen
bananas in chocolate to coat or
spoon chocolate over bananas,
allowing excess to drip off. Serve
immediately. (Remelt chocolate
mixture if necessary.) Wrap and
freeze leftover coated bananas.

Banana Custard Pudding   Butterscotch Custard Pudding   Chocolate Custard Pudding

Puddings&Custards

Nutritious puddings and custards help supply the family's daily requirement of milk and eggs in an appealing form. For a party, serve them in a parfait or wine glass and top or layer with fruit or a dessert sauce.

Microwaving makes puddings and custards easy to make. It eliminates much of the stirring, and you can cook in a 4-cup measure. For a velvety texture, see How to Make Smooth Cream Fillings, page 112.

Vanilla Custard Pudding or Cream Pie Filling

½ cup sugar
2 tablespoons cornstarch
1 tablespoon flour
¼ teaspoon salt
2 cups milk

3 or 4 egg yolks, slightly beaten*
2 tablespoons butter or
   margarine, optional
1 teaspoon vanilla

Makes 6 servings

In 2- or 2½-qt. mixing bowl or casserole, combine sugar, cornstarch, flour and salt. Stir in milk. Microwave at High 7 to 10 minutes, or until thickened, stirring every 3 minutes.

Stir about ½ cup mixture into yolks. Return to mixture in casserole, stirring well. Microwave 1 to 2 minutes, or until thick. Stir in butter. Cool slightly and stir in vanilla. Cover to prevent skin from forming.

*2 whole eggs may be used. Increase flour to 2 tablespoons. For a pie filling use egg yolks, the filling makes a firm cut with soft sides. If a stiffer filling is desired, increase flour to 2 tablespoons. Use egg whites to make a meringue top.

Strawberry 'n Cream Pudding   Coffee Pecan Custard Pudding   Eggnog Custard Pudding

Variations:

Butterscotch Custard Pudding: Substitute packed brown sugar for granulated sugar. If desired, stir in ¼ cup chopped pecans with vanilla.

Banana Custard Pudding: Fold 2 sliced bananas into vanilla or chocolate pudding with vanilla.

Chocolate Custard Pudding: Increase sugar to ⅔ cup and add 2 ounces unsweetened chocolate to milk mixture. (Chocolate will melt when pudding is stirred. If not smooth, beat with rotary beater before adding yolks.)

Date Nut Custard Pudding: Use half brown sugar and add ½ cup cut-up dates before microwaving. Stir in ¼ cup chopped nuts with vanilla.

Coconut Custard Pudding: Stir ½ cup flaked coconut into mixture before microwaving. Add ¼ teaspoon almond extract with vanilla. (For pie, sprinkle meringue with coconut.)

Strawberry 'n Cream Pudding: Prepare Strawberry Sauce, page 144, and layer with Vanilla Custard Pudding in sherbet or parfait glasses.

Coffee Pecan Custard Pudding: Use half brown sugar and add 2 teaspoons powdered instant coffee to mixture before microwaving. Stir in ⅓ cup chopped pecans with vanilla.

Eggnog Custard Pudding: Use 4 egg yolks. Stir in 2 teaspoons rum flavoring and ¼ teaspoon nutmeg with vanilla. Serve topped with whipped cream and sprinkled with nutmeg.

Calorie Counter: Decrease sugar to ⅓ cup. Use skim milk and omit butter.

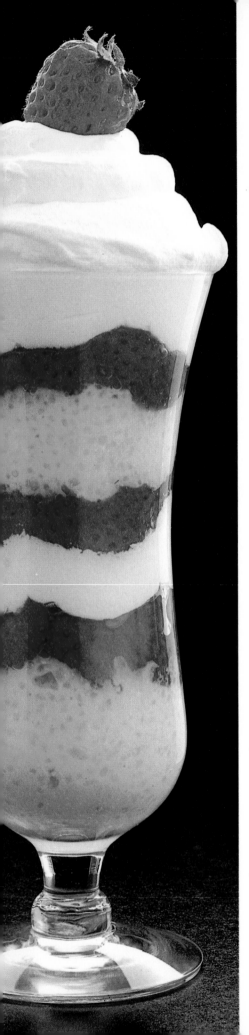

Tapioca Pudding

1 egg, separated
2 cups milk
3 tablespoons quick-cooking
   tapioca
5 tablespoons sugar, divided
¼ teaspoon salt
1 teaspoon vanilla

Makes 4 to 6 servings

In 1½-qt. casserole, blend egg yolk, milk, tapioca, 3 tablespoons sugar and salt. Let stand 5 minutes. Beat egg white in small bowl until foamy, gradually adding 2 tablespoons sugar. Beat until soft peaks form; set aside.

Stir tapioca mixture well. Microwave at High 4½ to 7½ minutes, or until mixture comes to full boil, stirring after 3 minutes, then every minute. Stir in vanilla. Fold in egg white. Let stand 15 minutes. Serve warm or cold.

Variation:

◀ **Tapioca Parfaits:** Layer cooled tapioca pudding, ¾ cup whipping cream and 1½ cups sliced fresh or frozen strawberries (10 oz. pkg., thawed, page 7) in parfait or sherbert dishes.

Chocolate Pots de Creme

1⅓ cups half & half
3 tablespoons sugar
  Pinch salt
1 cup chocolate chips
3 egg yolks
1 teaspoon vanilla

Makes 6 to 8 servings

In 4-cup measure or 1-qt. mixing bowl, combine half & half, sugar, salt and chips. Microwave at High 3 to 6 minutes, or just until boiling, stirring after 2 minutes, then every minute. Do not boil.

Beat yolks and vanilla until well blended and thickened. Gradually beat in chocolate mixture at low speed. Strain into pot de creme cups, small wine glasses or demitasse cups. Chill thoroughly. Serve topped with whipped cream, if desired.

Baked Custard

⅓ cup sugar
1 teaspoon cornstarch
2½ cups milk
1 teaspoon vanilla
⅛ teaspoon salt
4 eggs, beaten
Nutmeg

Makes 6 servings

In small bowl, combine sugar and cornstarch. Microwave milk in 4-cup measure or 1½-qt. casserole or bowl at High 2 to 4 mintues, or until very hot but not boiling. Blend sugar mixture, vanilla and salt into eggs at low speed. Stir into milk. Sprinkle with nutmeg.

Place casserole in baking dish; add ½-in. hot water around casserole. Microwave at 50% (Medium) 7 to 12 minutes, or until slightly firm but still soft in center, rotating ¼ turn every 2 minutes. Let stand at least 30 minutes before serving. Serve warm or chilled.

Bread Pudding

2½ cups milk
2 cups dry bread cubes or coarse crumbs
2 tablespoons cornstarch
½ cup raisins
⅓ cup sugar
½ teaspoon cinnamon
½ teaspoon vanilla
¼ teaspoon salt
3 eggs or 4 egg yolks, beaten

Makes 6 to 8 servings

Microwave milk in a 4-cup measure or small bowl at High 4 to 6 minutes, or until hot but not boiling. In 2-qt. casserole, toss bread, cornstarch, raisins, sugar, cinnamon, vanilla and salt. Gradually stir in milk, then eggs.

Microwave at High 2 minutes; stir carefully. Reduce power to 50% (Medium). Microwave 4 to 8 minutes, or until almost set in center, gently pushing outer edges toward center every 3 minutes. Do not overcook. Let stand directly on countertop at least 30 minutes before serving. Serve warm or cold, plain or with cream. If desired, sprinkle with cinnamon before serving.

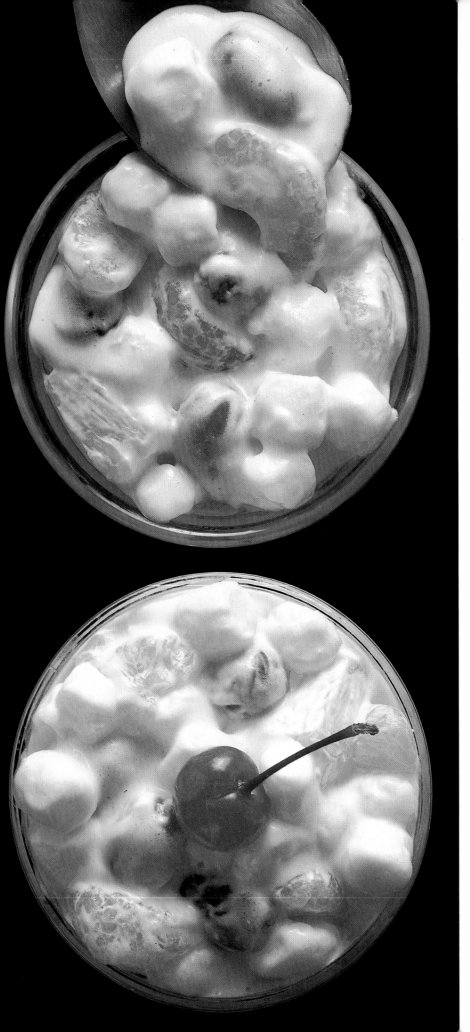

Refrigerator Desserts

Refrigerator desserts must be made in advance, so they're good choices for occasions when you want to avoid last minute cooking. Many can be stored several days.

Some refrigerator desserts are baked, cooled and chilled before serving. Others go into the refrigerator soft and firm up after several hours.

Easy Overnight Fruit Salad Dessert

    1 package (3 to 3⅝ oz.) vanilla pudding and pie filling
1¾ cups milk
    1 can (11 oz.) mandarin oranges, well drained
    1 can (20 oz.) pineapple chunks, well drained
    2 cups seedless grapes, banana slices* or apple chunks
    2 cups miniature marshmallows
    1 cup whipping cream, whipped, or 2 cups whipped cream substitute
    Maraschino cherries or strawberries

Makes 10 to 12 servings

Place pudding mix in 4-cup measure or 1½-qt. mixing bowl. Stir in about ⅓ cup milk until smooth, then add remaining milk. Microwave at High 3 minutes; stir. Microwave 1 to 4 minutes, stirring every minute, or until mixture boils. Refrigerate until cold.

In large bowl, combine pudding, fruit and marshmallows. Fold in whipped cream. Refrigerate at least 8 hours or overnight. Garnish with cherries or strawberries.

*If bananas are used, add at serving time.

Cherry Lemon Tarts

24 cupcake liners
  2 tablespoons butter or margarine
  1 cup graham cracker crumbs
  2 tablespoons sugar
  1 can (14 oz.) sweetened condensed milk
  2 eggs
  1 tablespoon grated lemon peel
⅓ cup lemon juice
  1 can (21 oz.) cherry pie filling

Makes 12 servings

Place 2 liners in each 5- or 6-oz. custard cup.* In small bowl, microwave butter at High 45 to 60 seconds, or until melted. Stir in crumbs and sugar. Place 1 rounded tablespoonful crumb mixture in each liner. Press down firmly with small glass. Blend remaining ingredients except pie filling until thickened. Place 2 tablespoons in each cup. Arrange 6 cups in ring in oven.

Microwave at 50% (Medium) 2 to 5 minutes, or just until each bubbles in 1 or 2 spots, rotating after half the time. Remove tarts as they appear done. Cool and serve topped with pie filling. (Extra pie filling can be warmed and served over ice cream.)

*To re-use custard cups, transfer baked tarts to muffin pan to cool. If less than 6 are microwaved at a time, allow 20 to 30 seconds per cup.

Creamy Orange Squares

1 recipe gingersnap or chocolate Cookie Crumb Crust, page 105
1 package (3 to 3⅝ oz.) vanilla pudding and pie filling
2 cups milk
1 package (3 oz.) orange gelatin
1 cup boiling water
1 can (11 oz.) mandarin oranges, well drained
1 cup whipping cream, whipped, or 2 cups whipped cream substitute

Makes 8 or 9 servings

Press all but ¼ cup crumbs in bottom of 8×8- or 9×9-in. baking dish. Microwave at High 1½ minutes, rotating after half the time.

Place pudding mix in 4-cup measure or 1½-qt. mixing bowl. Stir in about ⅓ cup milk until smooth, then add remaining milk. Microwave at High 3 minutes; stir. Microwave 2 to 6 minutes, stirring every minute, or until mixture boils; set aside. Dissolve gelatin in boiling water; stir into pudding with oranges. Refrigerate until thickened but not set.

Fold orange mixture into whipped cream. Spoon over crumb crust. Sprinkle with reserved crumbs. Refrigerate at least 4 hours, or until set.

NOTE: May be served as a fruit salad dessert without the crust.

Cheesecake

Crust:
¼ cup butter or margarine
1 cup graham cracker crumbs
2 tablespoons sugar

Filling:
2 packages (8 oz. each) cream
  cheese
⅔ cup sugar
¼ teaspoon salt
⅓ cup milk
2 tablespoons lemon juice
4 eggs

Makes 8 to 10 servings

Cheesecake Toppings:

Sour Cream Topping: Cool cheesecake 20 to 30 minutes, then spread with 1 cup dairy sour cream.

Fresh Fruit Topping: After chilling, top cheesecake with 1 to 2 cups fresh strawberries, raspberries, blueberries or sliced peaches.

Cherry Topping: Before chilling, spread 1 cup cherry pie filling over cheesecake. (Or use Strawberry Glaze, page 113.)

Glacé Topping: Combine ⅓ cup apricot, raspberry or other preserves and 1 tablespoon lemon juice. Drizzle over cheesecake before chilling.

How to Microwave Cheesecake

Microwave butter in 9-in. round baking dish 45 to 60 seconds, or until melted. Stir in crumbs and 2 tablespoons sugar.

Press firmly in bottom of dish. Microwave at High 1½ minutes, rotating after 1 minute.

Place cream cheese in bowl. Microwave at 50% (Medium) 1 minute, or until softened. Add sugar, salt and milk; beat well. Blend in juice and eggs.

Microwave at High 4 to 7 minutes, or until very hot, stirring well every 2 minutes. Pour over crust.

Microwave at 50% (Medium) 7 to 15 minutes, or until almost set in center; rotate ¼ turn every 3 minutes. Mixture firms up as it chills.

Cool, then refrigerate at least 8 hours or overnight. Serve as is or with one of the toppings, above.

Dessert Sauces

Sauces dress up many desserts: ice cream, pudding, gingerbread, fresh fruit, even leftover cake. Microwaving eliminates scorching, constant stirring and messy clean up.

Microwave sauces take only minutes to make. Hot sauces can be made just before serving or as early as the day before. Store them in the refrigerator and reheat the amount needed. To reheat a cup or more, microwave 1 minute, then add 30 seconds at a time, stirring every 30 seconds, until sauce is as warm as desired. Smaller amounts may need only 30 seconds.

Butterscotch Topping

1 cup packed brown sugar
2 tablespoons flour
¼ cup milk
2 tablespoons corn syrup
¼ cup butter or margarine
   Dash of nutmeg, optional

Makes about 1½ cups

In 1½-qt. mixing bowl, combine brown sugar and flour. Stir in milk and syrup, then butter. Microwave at High 2 to 4 minutes, or until mixture boils; stir well. Microwave 3½ minutes. Stir in nutmeg. Serve warm.

Easy Caramel Sauce

28 caramel candies (½ lb.)
¼ cup half & half or milk

Makes about 1 cup

Combine ingredients in 2-cup measure or small bowl. Microwave at High 2 to 4 minutes, or until melted, stirring every minute. Serve warm or cold.

Hot Fudge Topping

½ cup granulated sugar
½ cup packed brown sugar
3 tablespoons cocoa
2 tablespoons flour
⅛ teaspoon salt
⅔ cup milk
2 tablespoons light corn syrup
1 tablespoon butter or
   margarine
½ teaspoon vanilla

Makes about 1½ cups

In 4-cup measure or small bowl, combine sugars, cocoa, flour and salt. Stir in milk and syrup, then butter. Microwave at High 2 to 4 minutes, or until mixture boils; stir well. Microwave 2 to 5 minutes, or until desired thickness and a rich chocolate color, stirring every 1½ minutes. Stir in vanilla. Serve hot or at room temperature.

Praline Sauce

½ cup packed brown sugar
½ cup butter or margarine
2 tablespoons water

Makes about ¾ cup

Place ingredients in 4-cup measure or small bowl. Microwave at High 1 to 2 minutes, or until butter is almost melted. Stir with rubber spatula or wire whisk, until smooth. Microwave 1½ to 2½ minutes, or until mixture boils 1 minute. Serve warm. Good topped with Cinnamon-sugared Walnuts, page 153.

Variation:

Spun Sugar Topping: Decrease water to 1 tablespoon. Boil 2 minutes. Drizzle in thin stream over ice cream or cold desserts.

NOTE: To reheat leftover sauce, add 1 to 3 teaspoons water.

Quick Chocolate Sundae or Fondue Sauce

1 cup semi-sweet or milk
  chocolate chips
1 cup miniature marshmallows
¼ cup milk

Makes about 1 cup

Combine ingredients in 4-cup measure or small bowl. Microwave at High 2½ to 4½ minutes, or until mixture comes to full boil and is thick and smooth, stirring well every minute. If sauce is too thick, stir in more milk. Serve warm.

For Fondue Sauce: Serve with chunks or wedges of apples, bananas, pears, pineapple, angel food or sponge cake, or large marshmallows.

Strawberry Sauce

2 teaspoons cornstarch
1 package (10-oz.) frozen,
  sweetened strawberries,
  thawed*, page 7
1 tablespoon lemon juice
  Red food coloring, optional

Makes about 1⅓ cups

In 4-cup measure or small bowl, combine cornstarch and strawberry juice. Stir in strawberries. Microwave at High 2 to 5 minutes, or until clear and thickened, stirring every minute. Stir in lemon juice and food coloring. Serve warm or cold.

*Other frozen fruit may be substituted for the strawberries.

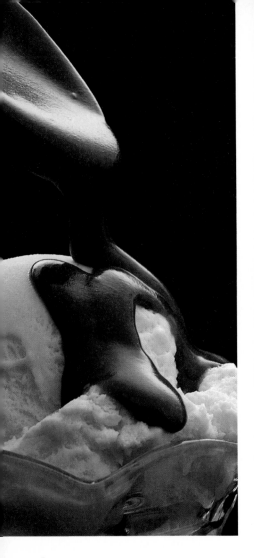

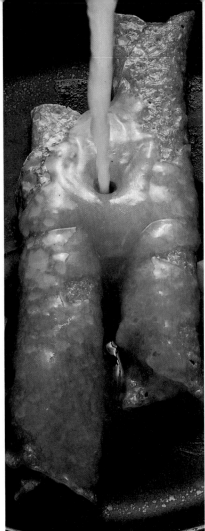

Short-cut Hot Fudge Peanut Sauce

1 cup milk chocolate or
    semi-sweet chocolate chips
¼ cup milk
¼ to ½ cup peanut butter

      Makes about 1¼ cups

Combine ingredients in 2-cup measure or small bowl. Microwave at 50% (Medium) 2 to 4 minutes, or until chips are soft. Stir with rubber spatula until well-blended. (If thinner sauce is desired, add more milk, a small amount at a time.) Serve warm or cold.

Sauce may be reheated at 50% (Medium) 30 to 60 seconds, depending on amount of sauce.

Orange Sauce

½ cup sugar
2 tablespoons cornstarch
  Pinch salt
1 cup boiling water
2 tablespoons butter or
  margarine
1 tablespoon grated orange
  peel
¼ cup orange juice
2 tablespoons lemon juice

      Makes about 1½ cups

In 4-cup measure or small bowl, combine sugar, cornstarch and salt. Stir in water and butter. Microwave at High 3 to 5 minutes, until clear and thickened, stirring after 2 minutes, then every minute. Stir in peel and juices. Serve warm on cake desserts, crepes and Plantation Dessert, page 128.

Lemon Butter Sauce

½ cup butter or margarine,
    room temperature
1 cup sugar
1 tablespoon cornstarch
1 tablespoon grated lemon peel
⅓ cup lemon juice
⅓ cup water
2 eggs, slightly beaten

      Makes about 2 cups

Cream butter, sugar and cornstarch. Blend in remaining ingredients. Microwave at High 3 to 6 minutes, or until clear and thickened, stirring after 2 minutes, then every minute. (Sauce may be made ahead and reheated.) Serve warm on gingerbread desserts, puddings and ice cream.

Variation:

Spoonable Lemon Topping:
Use 3 egg yolks or increase cornstarch to 2 tablespoons.

Hot Sauce with Fresh Fruit

½ cup packed brown sugar
1 tablespoon cornstarch
1 cup orange juice
2 tablespoons butter or
  margarine
1 tablespoon grated orange
  peel
2 tablespoons lemon juice
1 can (10-oz.) mandarin
  oranges, drained, or fresh
  grapes, halved
1 cup fresh or canned
  pineapple chunks
2 bananas, sliced

Makes about 4½ cups
(8 servings)

In 1½-qt. mixing bowl, combine brown sugar and cornstarch. Stir in orange juice and butter. Microwave at High 3 to 5 minutes, or until clear and slightly thickened, stirring after half the time. Stir in peel and lemon juice. Carefully stir fruit into hot sauce. (Sauce may be made ahead and reheated.) Serve over gingerbread or spice cake topped with whipped cream or ice cream, or serve as a hot fruit compote.

Sour Cream Sauce

½ cup packed brown sugar
½ cup dairy sour cream

Makes about 1 cup

Combine ingredients in 2-cup measure or small bowl. Microwave at 50% (Medium) 1 to 2 minutes, or until warm and brown sugar melts, stirring well after 1 minute. Serve warm over cake desserts, puddings, steamed puddings and many other desserts.

Candies

Both short-cut and old-fashioned cooked candies microwave easily with a minimum of stirring. Since candy syrups boil hard and can become very hot, use a large container which can withstand high temperatures. A bowl which has a handle is convenient. If a recipe calls for covering, use plastic wrap when a cover is not available.

Do not use a conventional candy thermometer in the microwave oven. Special microwave candy thermometers are available. If you do not have one, follow the cold water tests in the recipes.

Mallow Fudge

1 can (5⅔ oz.) evaporated milk
½ cup butter or margarine
2 cups sugar
1 jar (7 oz.) marshmallow creme

2 cups semisweet chocolate chips
½ cup chopped nuts, optional

Makes about 36 pieces

In 3-qt. casserole, combine milk, butter and sugar. Microwave at High 9 to 12 minutes, or until soft ball forms when small amount is dropped in cold water, stirring every 3 minutes.

Remove cover from creme. Microwave in jar at 50% (Medium) 30 seconds, or until softened. Stir into sugar mixture with chips and nuts until well blended. Pour into buttered or wax paper-lined 9×9-in. pan or dish. Let stand or refrigerate until firm. Cut into 1½-in. squares.

Chocolate Cobblestones

1 lb. chocolate confectioners' or
    candy coating
2 tablespoons shortening
1 cup salted peanuts
2 cups miniature marshmallows

Makes about 1½ lbs.
(36 pieces)

If candy coating is in solid piece, break into squares. Place in single layer in 2-qt. casserole with shortening. Microwave at 50% (Medium) 3 to 5 minutes, or until pieces are soft, stirring after 3 minutes.

Stir in peanuts, then marshmallows, using as few strokes as possible. Spread on wax paper to 9-in. square. Let stand until firm. Cut into 1½-in. squares.

Nut Yummies

1 lb. vanilla confectioners' or
    candy coating
¼ cup milk
1½ cups salted peanuts
¾ lb. chocolate candy coating*

Makes about 3 dozen

If vanilla candy coating is in solid piece, break into squares. Place in single layer in 2-qt. casserole. Microwave at 50% (Medium) 3 to 5 minutes, or until soft, stirring after 3 minutes. Stir in milk and peanuts. Drop by rounded measuring teaspoonfuls onto wax paper, flattening each to ¼- to ½-in., if necessary. Let stand until firm.

Break chocolate candy coating into squares; place in small mixing bowl. Microwave as directed above for white candy coating. (If too thick, add 1 tablespoon shortening.) Dip each piece candy into chocolate coating to cover completely, using 1 or 2 forks. Let stand on wax paper until firm.

*1 cup chocolate chips may be substituted. See page 7 for melting instructions. If chocolate-flavored chips are used, melt with 2 tablespoons shortening.

Sponge Candy

1 cup sugar
1 cup dark corn syrup
1 tablespoon vinegar
1 tablespoon soda

Makes about 1 lb.

NOTE: Sponge Candy is a hard candy best made when humidity is low. Pieces can be dipped into melted chocolate. See page 7 for melting chocolate.

How to Microwave Sponge Candy

Combine sugar, syrup and vinegar, in 2-qt. mixing bowl or casserole. Cover and microwave at High 3 minutes; stir well.

Microwave uncovered at High 4½ to 10 minutes, until thickened (300°F.). Test by dropping small amount in cold water.

Remove threads from water. If threads bend, microwave a little longer. Candy is done if threads are very brittle.

Quickly stir in soda; mix well. Mixture will foam up as soda is stirred in.

Pour into buttered foil-lined 8×8- or 9×9-in. baking dish, allowing mixture to spread itself.

Let stand until firm. Remove from dish and break into pieces.

Caramel Nut Rolls

½ lb. caramel candies
    (about 28)
¼ cup butter or margarine
2 tablespoons half & half or
    milk
1½ cups confectioners' sugar
1 cup salted peanuts
2 cups miniature
    marshmallows
1 cup flaked coconut

Makes about 2 lbs.
(48 pieces)

In 2-qt. casserole or mixing
bowl, place caramels, butter and
half & half. Microwave at 50%
(Medium) 3 to 5 minutes, or until
melted and smooth, stirring after
2 minutes, then every minute.

Stir in sugar until smooth, then
peanuts. Stir in marshmallows,
using as few strokes as possible.
Sprinkle 2 large sheets of wax
paper with coconut. Spoon half
the caramel mixture in strip on
each sheet. Shape into 10- or
12-in. rolls, using wax paper to
help shape; coat well with
coconut. Wrap and refrigerate.
To serve, cut into ½-in. slices.

Light Caramels

2 cups sugar
¾ cup light corn syrup
¼ cup butter or margarine
1¾ cups whipping cream,
    divided
    Pinch salt
1 teaspoon vanilla
1 cup chopped walnuts or
    other nuts, optional

Makes about 2 lbs. (36 pieces)

In 3-qt. casserole, combine
sugar, syrup, butter, 1 cup
cream and salt. Microwave at
High 10 minutes, stirring twice.
Gradually stir in ¾ cup cream.
Microwave 15 to 19 minutes, or
until hard ball forms (250°F.)
when small amount is dropped in
cold water. Stir every 3 or 4 minutes the first 15 minutes, then
every 1 or 2 minutes. (When cooked, mixture will be caramel color.)

Stir in vanilla and nuts. Pour into
buttered foil-lined 8×8-in. pan.
Let stand until firm. Remove from
pan. Cut into 1-in. squares. Wrap
in plastic wrap.

NOTE: If mixture separates while
cooking, beat until smooth with
wire whisk or rotary beater.

Hand-dipped Creams

Cream:
1 lb. confectioners' or candy
coating, any flavor
¼ cup vegetable shortening

Coating:
½ lb. confectioners' or candy
coating, any flavor
1 tablespoon shortening

Makes about 1½ lbs.
(36 squares)

Variations for Creams:

Stir one of the following into
melted cream mixture.

¾ to 1 cup chopped nuts,
peanuts, flaked coconut or
raisins
1 teaspoon peppermint or mint
flavoring
½ cup peanut butter
2 cups ready-to-eat cereal
½ cup peanut butter and 2 cups
ready-to-eat cereal
1 teaspoon maple flavoring

NOTE: For a more attractive
appearance, use different flavor
candy coatings for the cream
and the dip. However, a white
dip does not work well with a
dark candy.

How to Microwave Hand-dipped Creams

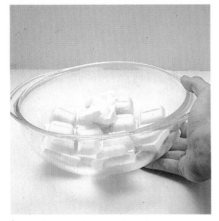

Break candy coating into
squares if it is in solid piece.
Place 1 lb. in single layer in 2-qt.
casserole with ¼ cup shortening. Microwave at 50% (Medium)
3 to 5 minutes, or until pieces are
soft; stir after 3 minutes.

Spread in wax paper-lined loaf
dish. Let stand just until firm in
center. Cut into 1-in. squares; let
harden completely.

Place ½ lb. candy coating in
small bowl with shortening.
Microwave as directed for
creams. Dip each square into
candy coating to cover
completely, using 1 or 2 forks.
Let stand on wax paper until firm.

Granola Crunch

½ cup butter or margarine
¾ cup packed brown sugar
¼ cup honey
¼ cup water
1 teaspoon salt
½ teaspoon cinnamon
3 cups old-fashioned oats
1 cup sunflower seed or almond
  slices
1 cup wheat germ
1 cup flaked coconut, optional*

Makes 2 lbs.

In 2½- or 3-qt. casserole,
combine butter, sugar, honey,
water, salt and cinnamon. Microwave at High 5 to 8 minutes, or
until slightly thickened, stirring
after 4 to 6 minutes.

Stir in remaining ingredients.
Reduce power to 50%
(Medium). Microwave 8 to 12
minutes, or until rich golden
brown, stirring after 3 to 6
minutes, then every 2 minutes.
Spread on buttered cookie
sheet, pressing down lightly with
pancake turner. Let stand until
firm. Break into small pieces and
store in airtight container.

*Raisins may be substituted; stir
in after microwaving.

Cinnamon-sugared Walnuts

½ cup sugar
½ cup packed brown sugar
½ cup water
½ teaspoon cinnamon
½ teaspoon vanilla
2 cups walnut halves or other
  nuts

Makes 3 cups
(scant lb.)

In 3-qt. mixing bowl or
casserole, combine sugars,
water and cinnamon. Cover and
microwave at High 3 minutes;
stir well. Microwave uncovered 5
to 8 minutes, or until soft ball
forms when small amount is
dropped in cold water.*

Stir in vanilla and walnuts until
coating sugars. Spread on wax
paper. Let stand until firm. Store
in airtight container.

*If mixture boils near top of dish,
open oven door occasionally to
slow down boiling.

Copy Pop

1 cup butter or margarine
½ cup light corn syrup
1¼ cups sugar
2 quarts salted popped corn
1½ to 2 cups nuts*
1 teaspoon vanilla

Makes 12 cups

In 2- or 2½-qt. mixing bowl or
casserole, combine butter,
syrup and sugar. Microwave at
High 9 to 15 minutes, or until
brittle threads form when small
amount is dropped in cold water,
stirring every 3 minutes.

In buttered 5-qt. (or larger)
container, combine corn and
nuts. Stir vanilla into cooked
syrup and immediately pour
over corn mixture. Stir with meat
fork until well coated. Spread
mixture in single layer on 2 large
sheets of wax paper. Let stand
until firm. Break into small pieces
and store in airtight container.

*Use walnut or pecan halves,
whole almonds, salted peanuts
or a combination.

Index